MW01129273

ANGEL

volume one

scriptbook

Issue #1: "City Of"
Written by Joss Whedon & David Greenwalt

Issue #2: "A Hole In The World"
Written by Joss Whedon

Issue #3: "Waiting In The Wings"
Written by Joss Whedon

Issue #4: "Spin The Bottle"
Written by Joss Whedon

Issue #5: "Five By Five"
Written by Jim Kouf

Spot illustrations by Jeff Johnson

Book design by Neil Uyetake

Collection edits by Justin Eisinger

Original series edited by Chris Ryall

Original series book design by Robbie Robbins

Production Assist by Chance Boren

www.idwpublishing.com   Photo cover by Frank Ockenfels III

ANGEL created by Joss Whedon and David Greenwalt • Thanks to Debbie Olshan at Fox Worldwide Publishing for her invaluable assistance.

IDW Publishing is:
Ted Adams, Co-President
Robbie Robbins, Co-President
Kris Oprisko, Vice President
Chris Ryall, Publisher/Editor-in-Chief
Neil Uyetake, Art Director
Dan Taylor, Editor
Justin Eisinger, Editorial Assistant
Chris Mowry, Production Assistant
Matthew Ruzicka, CPA, Controller
Alonzo Simon, Shipping Manager
Alex Garner, Creative Director
Yumiko Miyano, Business Development
Rick Privman, Business Development

ANGEL SCRIPTBOOK, VOLUME 1, TPB, NOVEMBER 2006. FIRST PRINTING. Angel is © 2006 Twentieth Century Fox Film Corporation. All Rights Reserved. © 2006 Idea and Design Works, LLC. The IDW logo is registered in the U.S. Patent and Trademark Office. All Rights Reserved. IDW Publishing, a division of Idea and Design Works, LLC. Editorial offices: 4411 Morena Blvd., Suite 106, San Diego, CA 92117. Any similarities to persons living or dead are purely coincidental. With the exception of artwork used for review purposes, none of the contents of this publication may be reprinted without the permission of Idea and Design Works, LLC. Printed in Korea
IDW Publishing does not read or accept unsolicited submissions of ideas, stories, or artwork.

ANGEL

issue one

scriptbook

Episode
CITY OF

Written By
JOSS WHEDON & DAVID GREENWALT

ANGEL™
"CITY OF"

WRITTEN BY

JOSS WHEDON
&
DAVID GREENWALT

Starring:
DAVID BOREANAZ
CHARISMA CARPENTER
GLENN QUINN

Created By
JOSS WHEDON
&
DAVID GREENWALT

Guest Starring:
TRACY MIDENDORF
VYTO RUGINIS
CHRISTIAN KANE

Consulting Producer
MARTI NOXON

Producer
TRACEY STERN

Producer
TIM MINEAR

Producer
KELLY A. MANNERS

Produced By
GARETH DAVIES

Executive Producers
SANDY GALLIN
GAIL BERMAN

Executive Producers
FRAN RUBEL
KAZ KUZUI

Consulting Producer
HOWARD GORDON

Written By
JOSS WHEDON & DAVID GREENWALT

Directed By
JOSS WHEDON

A N G E L
"CITY OF"

WRITTEN BY
JOSS WHEDON
&
DAVID GREENWALT

1 EXT. THE CITY - NIGHT

AERIAL SHOTS - We move across the city… tall buildings jut into the sky...
freeways over-and-under-lap one another, it's big and cold and fast here...

>   ANGEL (V.O.)
>   Los Angeles. It's a city like no other... And like all
>   others.

We see various contrasting shots: the glamour of Hollywood, the downtown poor,
ethnic neighborhoods... the different L.A.s.

>   ANGEL (cont'd; V.O.)
>   It has a hundred faces, each different, each one
>   beckoning.

2 EXT. DOWNTOWN STREET - NIGHT

Bums drink, beg, well-dressed men and women head from the high rise offices
towards bars and cars. CAMERA PUSHES IN ON a downtown bar and we hear:

>   ANGEL (V.O.)
>   People are drawn here. People, and other things. They
>   come for all kinds of reasons. My reason? It started
>   with a girl.

3 INT. DOWNTOWN BAR - NIGHT

The joint is happening: artists from the downtown lofts, young
professionals, unemployed actors on the make, etc. We DOLLY towards
the bar where the SERIOUS DRINKERS live.

>   ANGEL (V.O.)
>   ...A really really pretty girl.

At the bar we discover ANGEL himself -- drinking and talking to someone next to
him. He is clearly SOUSED.

>   ANGEL
>   No, I mean she was a hottie girl. She had... her hair
>   was... You know, you kind of remind me of her.

CAMERA WIDENS -- Angel is speaking to a LARGE BLACK MAN who is drinking and
ignoring him.

>   ANGEL (cont'd)
>   ...'cause, you know, the hair... I mean you both have
>   hair...

A woman's laugh draws Angel's gaze to three GOOD LOOKING GUYS shooting pool
with TWO GOOD LOOKING YOUNG WOMEN nearby. They're laughing, having a good time.
One of the guys gets behind one of the women (JANICE, who may resemble Buffy)
helping her line up a shot.

Another (GOOD LOOKING GUY #1) comes to the bar and squeezes in next to Angel. He
hands the bartender a fifty.

                    GOOD LOOKING GUY # 1
          (to the bartender)
          We're gonna cash out.

Angel smiles at him stupidly.

                    ANGEL
          Girls are nice.

The guy stares at him a moment, then collects his change and splits.

ANGLE - The three GUYS and the TWO GIRLS move past Angel, heading out the back
exit. As they do, he swivels slowly around on his stool, watching them. CAMERA
PUSHES IN as his whole demeanor changes. His eyes go cold and purposeful, his
loopy expression sober and focussed.

He isn't drunk, he's a man with a mission.

4 EXT. PARKING LOT BEHIND BAR - NIGHT

Fairly dark and deserted. Janice, her friend and the three guys move through.

                    JANICE
          You guys really know the doorman, you can get us in
          the Lido?

                    GOOD LOOKING GUY # 1
          I don't want to go clubbing anymore.
          (throws his arm around her)
          I want to party right here.

                    JANICE
          Hey, back off.

                    GOOD LOOKING GUY # 1
          "Hey", shut up and die.

And he GROWLS and MORPHS INTO A TERRIFYING, YELLOW-EYED, FANG-TOOTHED VAMPIRE.
He grabs Janice as Guys # 2 & 3 swing around (VAMP FACED) and grab her
friend. The women are too freaked to even scream as Angel stumbles into frame,
apparently snockered.

                    ANGEL
          'Scusey, scusey, anybody seen my car? It's big and
          shiny... (looks around) ...why does it keep doing this
          to me?

                    GOOD LOOKING GUY # 1
          (in shadow) Piss off, pal.

Angel stumbles up to the guy. Looks up at him and registers drunken shock at his
face. Brow furrowed. Angel digs in his coat pocket -- and pulls out some dental
floss.

                    ANGEL
          No. I want you to have it.

Guy # 1 shoves Janice to the side -- she hits her head against the wall -- and
comes for Angel who drops the drunk act and whips his elbow up under Guy # 1's
chin, knocking him clean over a car as -- # 2 charges and Angel spin kicks him,
but gets clocked from the side by # 3. Angel and # 3 trade vicious blows. Angel
sends him crashing into a pile of garbage, splintering some boxes in the fall.

10

Laura and Janice (holding her bleeding head) watch, as --

2 gets to his feet and charges, # 3 gets to his feet and does the same. Angel stands there, waiting calmly and efficiently -- they come at him from either side. He holds his hands down behind his back, and TWO SHARP WOODEN STAKES (attached to hidden spring devices on his wrists) RATCHET into his hands. He shoots his arms out to either side, nailing them both simultaneously. # 2 and # 3 explode in a cacophony of dust.

Angel de-ratchets his stakes. He hears footsteps, swings around as # 1 rears up
with a metal trash can and bashes him in the face with it. Angel hits the
ground hard -- his back to Laura and Janice, who don't see his face.

                              ANGEL (cont'd)
                    You shouldn't have done that.

Angel grabs # 1 -- who is shocked to see that Angel has gone vampfaced -- and
beats the crap out of him, finally flinging him head first into a Mercedes
windshield, knocking him out and setting off the CAR ALARM.

In the calm, Janice approaches Angel from behind.

                              JANICE
                    Oh my god, you saved our lives...

His back to them, he walks away.

                              ANGEL
                    Go home.

                              JANICE
                    (heads after him)
                    They were... oh god... thank you --

She grabs his arm. Pulling him around, seeing his VAMP FACE. He sees a tiny
trickle of blood (from where she hit her cheek) edging down her neck. He looks
at her blood as only a drowning man can.

                              ANGEL
                    Get away from me.

She reacts, quickly backs away with Laura.

Angel walks toward us, grim and dark, the women getting in their car in b.g.
Without breaking stride, Angel grabs a broken stake from the trash and DUSTS the
semi-conscious vamp sprawled on the car hood. He MORPHS back to human, walking
into a BIG ASS CLOSE-UP -- and then into darkness.

                         END OF TEASER

                           ACT ONE

5 EXT. L.A. STREETS - NIGHT

Old L.A., mostly BUMS and DRUGGIES on the boulevard at this hour. Angel walks
past, keeping to himself like everyone else on the street...

Angel turns up a smaller street, a mix of old residential and small commercial
buildings. He enters:

6 INT. ANGEL'S BUILDING - NIGHT

Old offices on the ground floor, apartments above. Angel unlocks a door and we
FOLLOW him:

7 INT. OFFICE - NIGHT

An outer and inner office space, not in use, beat-up desk, chairs and a couple of musty filing cabinets shoved into corners. Angel locks the door behind him (with dead bolt and security plate), moves through; in the back corner, an old elevator. He enters the elevator, pushes DOWN.

8 INT. ANGEL'S APT. - NIGHT

The elevator door opens. Angel enters his basement apartment. Not a huge space but clean and eclectically elegant with Angel's furniture, tapestries and art.

9 INT. STUDY - CONTINUOUS

Arcane books, some easy chairs, and off to one side an array of weapons.

Angel enters, then slips off his coat, tosses it on a chair. He undoes the two ratchet-stake devices strapped to his forearms, drops them on a table where we see other stakes, knives, a fighting ax.

Angel leans on the table, staring at the weaponry, alone and brooding. Then, sensing a presence, he turns slowly and sees DOYLE (gambler, hustler, Irish accent), standing in the doorway.

                    DOYLE
          Well, I like the place. Not much with the view, but
          it's got a nice Batcave sort of air to it.

                    ANGEL
          Who are you?

                    DOYLE
          Doyle. And, no, we haven't met before, so don't be
          embarrassed.

                    ANGEL
          I'm not. You don't smell human.

                    DOYLE
          Well, that's a bit rude. As it happens I'm very much
          human...

He sneezes -- and suddenly MORPHS into a blue, scaly thing. Shakes it off, human again...

                    DOYLE (cont'd)
          ... on my mother's side. Anyway I come in uninvited so
          you know I'm not a vampire like yourself.

He starts in, crossing past Angel to the weapons.

                    ANGEL
          What do you want?

                    DOYLE
          I been sent. By the powers that be.

                         ANGEL
          The powers that be what?

                         DOYLE
          This is an exciting bunch of crimefighting devices.

He picks up a throwing star.

                         DOYLE (cont'd)
          I can't believe you really know how to use these.

                         ANGEL
          (glowering) I'm anxious to show you.

                         DOYLE
          Tell you something, friend: I'm about as happy to be
          here as you are to see me. But there's work to be
          done, and we got the call. Let me tell you a little
          bedtime story.

                         ANGEL
          But I'm not sleepy.

                         DOYLE
          Once upon a time, there was a vampire, and he was the
          meanest vampire in all the land. Other vampires were
          afraid of him, he was such a bastard. A hundred years
          this guy's killing and maiming and such like. Then one
          day, he's cursed. By gypsies. They restore his human
          soul and all of a sudden he's mad with guilt, "what
          have I done", very freaked. So he sulks about for
          another hundred years...

                         ANGEL
          Okay. I'm sleepy.

                         DOYLE
          Well, it's a fairly dull tale. It needs a little sex,
          is my feeling, and sure enough, enter the girl. Pretty
          little blonde thing, Vampire Slayer by trade, and our
          vampire falls madly in love with her. And it's good,
          he makes something of himself, fights some evil, but
          then... eventually, the two of them, they get fleshy
          with one another, and the moment he... well, the
          technical term is "Perfect happiness", and as soon as
          our boy gets there, he goes bad again. Kills again.
          It's ugly. So when he gets his soul back a second
          time, he figures he can't be anywhere near young Miss
          Puppy Thighs without endangering them both. So he
          takes off. Goes to L.A., to fight evil and atone for
          his crimes. He's a shadow, a faceless champion of the
          hapless human race. Have you got a beer of any kind
          in here?

                         ANGEL
          No.

                         DOYLE
          You must have something besides pig's blood.

He crosses to the fridge, opens it as Angel speaks.

                              ANGEL
              Okay, you've told me the story of my life, which since
              I was there, I already knew. Why aren't I kicking you
              out?

                              DOYLE
              'Cause now I'm gonna tell you what happens next.

He closes the fridge, emptyhanded.

                              DOYLE (cont'd)
              See this vampire, he thinks he's helpin'. Fighting the
              demons, keeping away from the humans so as not to be
              tempted...
                      (indicates apartment)
              ... doing penance in his little cell.

He starts toward Angel, never taking his eyes off him.

                              DOYLE
              But he's cut off. From everything. From the people
              he's helping; they're not people to him at all,
              they're just the victims, statistics. Just numbers.

                              ANGEL
              I still save them. Who cares if I don't stop to chat?

                              DOYLE
              When was the last time you drank blood?

Angel has trouble answering...

                              DOYLE (cont'd)
              It was her. Your slayer friend -- Muffy, is it?

                              ANGEL
              I was sick. Dying. She fed me to cure me.

                              DOYLE
              Left you with a bit of a craving, didn't it? Well that
              craving is gonna grow. And someday soon one of those
              helpless victims you don't really care about will look
              too appetizing to turn down. And you'll figure,
              "what's one against all I've saved? I might as well
              eat 'em; I'm still ahead by the numbers."

He stares Angel down. Angel knows the truth of Doyle's words.

                              DOYLE (cont'd)
              Come on. I'm parched from all this yakkin'. Let's go
              treat me to a Billy D.

10 EXT. ANGEL'S STREET - NIGHT

Angel and Doyle exit a 24 hour liquor store. Doyle is drinking a 40 ounce malt
liquor in a paper bag.

                              DOYLE
              Ah, that's good drink. I will pay you back, I'm just a
              little pressed for cash this week.

ANGEL
So what do I do? I assume you came here with some
alternative. How do I change things?

DOYLE
You got to mix it up. Get in there with the humans.
It's not all fighting and gadgets and such. It's about
reaching out to people, caring about them, about
showing them there's hope in this world -- (to a
begging woman) -- Get a JOB, you lazy sow -- (to
Angel) --about letting them in your heart. It's not
just about saving lives, it's about saving souls --
possibly your own in the process.

ANGEL
(beat; taking that in)
I wanna know who sent you.

DOYLE
I'm honestly not sure. They don't speak to me direct.
I get visions, which is to say great splitting
migraines that come with pictures. A name, a face. I
don't know who sends 'em. I just know whoever it is is
more powerful than you or me, and they're trying to
make things right.

ANGEL
Why me?

DOYLE
'Cause you got potential. And the balance sheet ain't
exactly in your favor just yet.

ANGEL
Why you?

DOYLE
(suddenly serious)
We all got something to atone for.

Angel lets it drop. Doyle fishes a piece of paper out of his
pocket.

DOYLE (cont'd)
Had a vision this morning. When the blinding pain
stopped, I wrote this down.

ANGEL
(reads)
"Tina. The Coffee Spot."

DOYLE
Nice looking girl. Needs help.

ANGEL
Help with what?

DOYLE
That's your business. I just get the names.

ANGEL
I don't get it. How am I supposed to know what she --

                    DOYLE
          You get involved, remember? Get into her life. High
          school's over, boy. Make with the grown-up talk.

                    ANGEL
          Why would a woman I've never met even talk to me?

                    DOYLE
          Have you looked in a mirror lately? (duh) No, I guess
          you really haven't.

A beat. Angel knows what he has to do, but...

                    ANGEL
          I'm not good with people.

                    DOYLE
          Well, that's the point of this little exercise, isn't
          it? Get to know her. If you can help her, you'll both
          be the better for it. You game?

Off Angel's face...

11 EXT. THE CITY - NIGHT - SPECIAL FX

The lights of the cars zoom past in that impossibly fast *Koyaanisqatsi* way. The
sun roars into the sky in the same manner.

12 INT. ANGEL'S APT. - DAY

CLOSE - The slip of paper: TINA, COFFEE SPOT, S.M. scribbled on it. ANGEL
studies it for a long moment. Then suddenly he tosses it on the bedtable and
stands, moves out of frame.

MATCH CUT:

13 EXT. SANTA MONICA STREETS/COFFEE SPOT - NIGHT

Angel drives into frame behind the wheel of his car. THE CAR - pulls up in
front of THE COFFEE SPOT.

14 INT. COFFEE SPOT - NIGHT

Think Starbucks. Angel enters, looks around. YUPPIES sip and chat. UNIFORMED
EMPLOYEES (white shirts, black pants) work the registers and the coffee makers.

Angel stands apart sipping his coffee. He hears Tina talking to the MANAGER,
looks over.

                    MANAGER
          Tina, I gotta do it by seniority. Everyone wants to
          work extra hours.

                    TINA
          I know, I just need... I'm good for Saturday nights,
          if other people wanna go out... I'll double shift,
          whatever.

                    MANAGER
          You're on the list. Okay?

                              TINA
                  (deflated) Thanks.

She grabs a bus rag, heading in Angel's general direction. He steps forward like
he might say something to her.

She glances at him -- he can't think of anything to say, he just looks away and
sips his coffee -- she moves on to clean up a service area in b.g.

Angel sees a GUY with a cute and friendly dog. A couple of YOUNG WOMEN passing
by pet and coo over the dog.

Angel sees Tina heading back towards the counter. He edges to the dog, holds out
his hand to pet him.

                              ANGEL
                  Sure is a cute little...

Tina, moving past, doesn't get that he's talking to her -- the cute and friendly
dog backs away from Angel and lies down, cowed.

                              ANGEL (cont'd)
                  ...doggie.

Now he feels really out of place. Tina clears the table next to her. Angel tries
again.

                              ANGEL (cont'd)
                  Do you, uh, how late are you open?

                              TINA
                  Are you talking to me?

She looks up as she says it -- and inadvertently knocks a full mug of coffee
off the edge of the table.

                              TINA (cont'd)
                  Oh!

THE FULL CUP is caught halfway to the floor by Angel who hands it back to Tina.

                              TINA (cont'd)
                  Wow. Good reflexes.

Angel nods, still can't think of what to say.

                              TINA (cont'd)
                  Well, thanks. These come out of my paycheck.

                              ANGEL
                  So, are you... happy?

                              TINA
                  What?

                              ANGEL
                  You looked sort of... down.

                              TINA
                  You been watching me?

>   ANGEL
>   No, I just, I was looking towards there... and you
>   walked through there...

She smiles, disarmed by his genuine artlessness.

>   TINA
>   You don't hit on girls very often, do you?

>   ANGEL
>   It's been a while. I'm sort of new in town.

>   TINA
>   Do yourself a favor. Don't stay.

She starts to leave.

>   ANGEL
>   You never answered my question.

>   TINA
>   Am I happy? You got three hours?

>   ANGEL
>   Do I look busy?

She pauses, considers.

>   TINA
>   I get off at ten.

15 EXT. COFFEE SPOT - NIGHT

Tina, wearing a nice dress, large carry bag over her shoulder, walks with
purpose towards Angel, leaning against his car.

>   ANGEL
>   I suddenly feel underdressed. Did you want to get a
>   drink, or --

She holds up her key ring, pointing a tube of MACE at him.

>   TINA
>   I know who you are, what you're doin' here. You stay
>   the hell away from me and you tell Russell to leave me
>   alone.

>   ANGEL
>   I don't know anyone named Russell.

>   TINA
>   You're lying.

>   ANGEL
>   No I'm not.

>   TINA
>   Then why were you in there watching me?

                              ANGEL
              Because you looked lonely.
              (beat)
              And I figured, then we have something in common.

She looks at him for a long beat, then she lowers the mace.

                              TINA
              I'm sorry. I'm really...

                              ANGEL
              It's okay.

                              TINA
              No it's not... I'm sort of having "relationship
              issues". You probably guessed that.

                              ANGEL
              Who's Russell?

She just shakes her head.

                              ANGEL (cont'd)
              I'd like to help.

                              TINA
              Only help I need is a ticket home, and that wasn't me
              asking for money. I've taken... money before. Never
              comes free.

                              ANGEL
              Where's home?

                              TINA
              Missoula, Montana. You ever been to Missoula?

                              ANGEL
              During the Depression.
              (catches himself)
              Er, my depression. I was depressed there. But it's
              pretty country.

                              TINA
              Yeah... Lotta open land, lotta drunk cowboys. Came
              here to be a famous movie star, but, um, they weren't
              hiring. Met a lot of colorful people on the way,
              though, which is why I come armed.

                              ANGEL
              Fair enough.

                              TINA
              You kinda remind of the boys back home. 'cept you're
              not drunk.

                              ANGEL
              (deadpan)
              I'm high on life.

                              TINA
              Yeah, it's a kick.
              (smiles; checks watch)

Well... I gotta go to a fabulous Hollywood party.
(re: dress)
Hence the glamour. Girl giving it owes me my security
deposit. (not sure what else to say) Well. It was nice
threatening you.

                    ANGEL
          You need a lift?

She thinks a moment. Takes a step toward him,

                    TINA
          What's your name?

                    ANGEL
          Angel.

16 EXT. HIGH RISE APTS. - NIGHT

Angel's car (Angel and Tina inside) pulls up to the classy high rise and
disappears into the underground parking.

17 INT. HIGH RISE APT. - NIGHT

Nice place, city view, full of the YOUNG and HIP. MARGO (Tina plus five years of
hard living) opens the front door and aims her VIDEO CAM at Angel and Tina.

                    MARGO
          Smile for the camera. Who's this hunk of tall, dark
          and handsome?

                    TINA
          He's a friend... Margo, I really need to talk to you.

                    MARGO
          Get yourself a drink, I'll be there.

Margo turns the camera on other arriving GUESTS as Tina and Angel drift towards
the hors d'oeuvres table. Tina indicates the mountain of party sandwiches cut in
the shape of stars.

                    TINA
          Cute, everyone's a star.

                    ANGEL
          Who's Russell?

                    TINA
          You don't want to know.

                    ANGEL
          Actually I do.

                    TINA
          He's someone I made the mistake of trusting.

Margo moves up.

                    MARGO
          Here I am.

                              TINA
                    (to Angel)
                    This won't take long.

                              MARGO
                    (smiles at Angel)
                    I wouldn't leave that one unattended.

They move off. He looks around at the hip folks chatting and drinking, feeling
out of place.

He finds himself confronted by a tidy businessman (OLIVER) of about 45, who
stares at him intently.

                              OLIVER
                    You are a beautiful, beautiful man.

                              ANGEL
                    Uh... thanks.

                              OLIVER
                    You're an actor.

                              ANGEL
                    No.

                              OLIVER
                    (holds out his card)
                    It wasn't a question. I'm Oliver, ask anyone about
                    Oliver, they'll tell you that I am a fierce animal.
                    I'm your manager as soon as you call.

                              ANGEL
                    I'm not an actor.

                              OLIVER
                    Funny. I like the humor, I like the whole thing.
                    Spelling has a pilot going up, I don't know what it's
                    about but you're perfect. Call me, this is not a come
                    on, I'm in a very serious relationship with a
                    landscape architect.

He leaves. Angel has no idea what to say. He leaves the card on the table,
turns to look around some more - and hears a familiar laugh.

He rounds a corner to see CORDELIA talking to a couple of young suits.

                              CORDELIA
                    Oh, Calloway is a pig! I won't even read for him
                    anymore. How do you think Alexis got the part? Oh
                    please. There's a short walk between acting and
                    faking. Anyway she's way too old. It should be someone
                    fresh, you know, like a young Natalie Portman...

                              ANGEL
                    Cordelia.

She looks over at Angel. Clearly shocked to see him.

                              CORDELIA
                    Oh my God! Angel.

The suits drift away as she crosses to Angel. She clearly would rather be with them, but...

                              ANGEL
                    It's nice to see a familiar face.

                              CORDELIA
                    I didn't know you were in L.A. Are you living here?

                              ANGEL
                    Yeah. You?

                              CORDELIA
                    Malibu. Little condo on the beach. It's not a private
                    beach, but I'm young, so I forbear.

                              ANGEL
                    And you're acting?

                              CORDELIA
                    Can you believe it? I just started it as a way to make
                    some quick cash and then -- boom. It's my life. Lotta
                    work. I'm just trying to keep grounded, not let it go
                    to my head.

Awkward pause.

                              CORDELIA (cont'd)
                    So, are you still...
                    (makes claws and fangs)
                    ...Grrrr...?

                              ANGEL
                    Yeah. There's not actually a cure for that.

                              CORDELIA
                    Right. But you're not evil, you're not here to... you
                    know, bite people...

                              ANGEL
                    Just gave a friend a ride.

                              CORDELIA
                    Good. Isn't this a great party?

                              ANGEL
                    (not really)
                    Fabulous.

                              CORDELIA
                    So, who do you know?
                    (off his look)
                    Who do you know here? Somebody?

                              ANGEL
                    Just Tina. This isn't exactly my scene.

                              CORDELIA
                    Well, yeah, you're the only vampire here.

                              ANGEL
                    I kind of doubt that.

                              CORDELIA
                    Well, I better get mingly; I really should be talking
                    to the people who are somebody. But it was fun!

She leaves. Angel watches her, says to no one:

                              ANGEL
                    It's nice that she's grown as a person.

Angel sees Tina returning, not looking too happy. She is intercepted by a
THUGGISH MAN (STACEY) in a great suit. Angel watches them have a few words.
The man puts his hand on her arm, she wrenches it away, moves to Angel.

                              TINA
                    Of course she doesn't have the money yet. Can we get
                    out of here?

                              ANGEL
                    (re: Stacey)
                    Who's that?

                              TINA
                    Just a creep. Can we please go?

They head for the door. Stacey watches them go. He pulls out a small cell phone,
as --

18 INT. PARKING GARAGE BENEATH HIGH RISE - NIGHT

Two elevators. One opens. Angel and Tina step out. Three BIG GUYS IN SUITS are
waiting. Two of them (THUGS 1 & 2) grab Angel, hustle him back into the elevator
which closes on them as the third guy stands between Tina and escape and the
second elevator door snaps open, revealing Stacey.

                              STACEY
                    He just wants to see you, that's all.

                              TINA
                    Okay... no problem.

Stacey indicates a waiting BMW 750. Tina obediently heads for it, then takes off
running. They take off after her. She dodges between some parked cars, gets
grabbed from behind by Thug 3.

                              TINA (cont'd)
                    Let go of me! LET GO OF ME!

As they put her in the car --

BLACK OUT.

                              END OF ACT ONE

                              ACT TWO

19 INT PARKING GARAGE - NIGHT - CONTINUOUS

CAMERA BLASTS PAST the revving BMW (Thug 3 at the wheel, Stacey in back with
Tina) to the elevator doors. We HEAR sounds of a struggle inside. The doors open
and Angel heads out (the two thugs down and out on the floor behind him), sees

the BMW roaring away and takes off running in the opposite direction the BMW took.

Angel jumps up on a parked car and runs across several more parked cars. INTERCUT: BMW heading for the exit and ANGEL'S FEET bounding across the parked cars. Angel leaps over the last car and -- cool action hero that he is -- lands in a convertible. Problem is: it's the wrong convertible. He sees HIS CAR nearby.

                              ANGEL
                   Damn.

He scrambles out. THE BMW - screeches around a corner, clear shot for the exit.

ANGEL'S CAR - roars into frame from the opposite direction, going straight for the BMW.

CLOSE - Thug 3 behind the wheel, sees the caddie.

CLOSE - ANGEL, not slowing, stopping or turning.

Thug 3 chickens out at the last minute, yanks the wheel.

THE BMW - swerves into the concrete wall, grinds to a halt in a shower of sparks and scrunching metal.

ANGEL - is already running towards the BMW as Thug 3 gets out pulling a gun. Angel kicks the gun out of his hand, straight up in the air. Thug 3 looks up at the gun. Angel smashes him in the face, grabs the gun out of the air and shoves it in Stacey's (barreling out of the back seat) neck. Angel pulls Tina out.

                         STACEY
                   (to Angel)
                   I don't know who you are but you don't want to get
                   involved here, trust me.

                         ANGEL
                   Tina, get in the car.

She gets in.

                        STACEY
          You know what? I don't think you're gonna pull that
          trigger.

Angel punches him in the face. He's on the ground in an instant.

                        ANGEL
          Good call.

Angel gets in the car, Stacey staring balefully at him.

                        TINA
          Nice party, huh?

                        ANGEL
          Little too fabulous for me.

He slams the car into gear, roars out.

20 EXT. CRUMMY APT. BUILDING - NIGHT - ESTABLISHING

21 INT. CORDELIA'S CRUMMY APT. - NIGHT

A HAND irons a pretty party dress. The dress is picked up and hung in a
threadbare closet. We see Cordelia, in her slip, move from the closet to
the little bed, sit.

This is no Malibu condo.

She hits the PLAY button on her answer machine. The machine says: "YOU HAVE
ONE NEW MESSAGE."

                        JOE'S VOICE ON MACHINE
          Cordy, it's Joe at the agency. No luck... again. I'm
          having trouble booking auditions, the networks are
          saying they've seen enough of you. Which means it's
          time to take a little breather, let 'em forget they
          remember ya' so don't call -- you know, no need to
          call me, I'll buzz ya' if something changes. Bye.

The machine says: "YOU HAVE NO MORE MESSAGES." Cordy sits there for a long beat
then picks up a napkin, unwraps it, revealing two star-shaped sandwiches from
the party. She lifts one to her mouth, takes a bite, chews slowly looking out
the window at the dark city.

22 INT. ANGEL'S APT. - NIGHT

Tina, wearing a t-shirt over her black work pants, exits the bathroom, drops her
party dress in her large bag:

                        TINA
          My Girl Scout training, be prepared. I can live out of
          this for days if I have to.

                        ANGEL
          (proffering a cup)
          I made some tea.

                        TINA
          (takes it)
          Thanks.

                    ANGEL
Do you take milk and sugar?
(she nods)
'Cause I don't have those things. I don't get a lot of
visitors.

                    TINA
(re: his ancient weapons on wall or in case)
At least not ones you like.

                    ANGEL
(smiles)
I have relationship issues, too.

                    TINA
It's weird. The second you get out of high school,
it's like, "Time to choose. Who you gonna be?" And
you're not ready for that. So you make a choice, and
another, and then it's a blur 'til you stop and look
around and this is who you are. You feel like, "How
can my body be twenty-eight when I feel so old?"

                    ANGEL
I really know what you mean.

                    TINA
 Yeah. Two lonely people.
 (glances at bed)
 I guess this is the part where you comfort me. Not
 like you didn't earn it.

  She gives him a hard look, her emotions churning beneath
  the surface. He moves to her.

                    ANGEL
 No. This is the part where you have a safe place to
 stay while we figure things out.

                    TINA
You don't want to...?

                    ANGEL
You got enough people taking advantage right now.

 Her eyes fill with tears. She tries to brush them away.

                    TINA
 Boy are you ever in the wrong town.

  She sits on the couch, cries; he gives her some Kleenex.

                    TINA (cont'd)
   Thank you...

                    ANGEL
   Does Russell have a last name?

                    TINA
Yeah, but you don't need to know it. You've done
enough already. This is L.A., guys like him get away
with murder.

                              ANGEL
               Who'd he murder?

                              TINA
               (beat)
               I don't know... maybe nobody... he's got the bucks,
               likes to hang with starlets and such... he was nice at
               first -- I'm not an idiot, I know he's gonna want
               something in return -- I figured what the hell, at
               least I'd be eating good.

Angel moves to her.

                              ANGEL
               What does he want in return?

                              TINA
               He likes to... he likes pain. I mean he really does;
               he talks about it like it's a friend of his. And you
               don't leave him, he tells you when he's had enough.
               I knew a girl, Denise, she tried to get away, she
               disappeared off the face of the earth. He finds you.

                              ANGEL
               Not anymore.

TIME CUT

SAME SCENE - A LITTLE LATER

Angel covers Tina, sleeping now, with a blanket. He studies her for a moment,
then his eyes fall on her large bag.

THE BAG - is put on the table. Angel reaches in, pulls out her address book,
opens it, sees her own name and address on the first page, starts thumbing
through it. A BUSINESS CARD FALLS OUT. Angel looks at it: WOLFRAM & HART,
ATTORNEYS AT LAW (with their distinctive LOGO). He puts the card aside, keeps
thumbing until he finds what he's looking for.

INSERT - A NAME - (handwritten by Tina) DENISE PERKINS and a few phone numbers,
all crossed out.

Off Angel,

23 EXT. L.A. LIBRARY - NIGHT - ESTABLISHING

24 INT. L.A. LIBRARY - NIGHT

A cavernous space, deserted at this hour.

A COMPUTER SCREEN lights up. NEWSPAPER SITE. WIDEN, we see two other SCREENS are
already on. Angel sits before them, gathering data. Angel types into the news
site: MURDERS, YOUNG WOMEN.

ON COMPUTER SCREEN # 2 - Info is coming up in response to SEARCH: PERKINS,
DENISE.

It reads: ACTRESS, MEMBER S.A.G., A.F.T.R.A.; DANCER IN LAS VEGAS UNDER THE
NAMES LYLA WILLIAMS, LYLA JONES.

Angel types WILLIAMS, LYLA and JONES, LYLA in, hits SEARCH. ON COMPUTER SCREEN # 3 - Angel scrolls POLICE FILES. MONTAGE - INTERCUT ANGEL and what he's learning:

SCREEN 1 - VARIOUS BACK PAGE (as opposed to front page) HEADLINES: Unidentified woman found strangled... Hiker finds body in Angeles Crest Forest... Murder Victim Trashed in Dumpster...

SCREEN 2 - Angel looks at a photo of LYLA JONES, DANCER A.K.A. DENISE PERKINS. Dressed up in a Vegas costume.

SCREEN 3 - He scrolls through various MISSING PERSONS REPORTS and JANE DOES. Stops, scrolls back to one. CLOSER - This Jane Doe's stats: five foot ten, 115 pounds... IDENTIFYING MARKS: tattoo on left shoulder.

SCREEN 2 - He goes back to the Vegas Photo of Lyia Jones. She has a small flower tattoo on her left shoulder.

PUSH IN ON ANGEL and PRE-LAP:

> TINA (O.S.)
>> No...!

25 OMITTED

26 INT. ANGEL'S APT. - DAY

Angel emerges from the tunnel in his living room floor, hears Tina on the couch in the throes of a nightmare. Angel enters, moves to her.

> TINA
>> I can't...

> ANGEL
>> Tina --

She SCREAMS! arching up, clawing at his face, real horror in her eyes.

> TINA
>> No!!!

> ANGEL
>> It's all right, everything's all right.

She recognizes him, collapses in his arms.

> TINA
>> He was here...

> ANGEL
>> It's just a dream, it's okay now...

They hold each other, her face against his, her tears on his cheek.

> TINA
>> Don't let me go...

She holds on even tighter, rocking a little... then touching his hair, his face... he puts his hand up on hers, responding for a moment, then gently pulls back.

                        ANGEL
          Did your friend Denise have a tattoo on her left
          shoulder?

                        TINA
          (nods) A rose.

                        ANGEL
          I think she was murdered... and there've
          been others. He picks girls with no
          families, no one to care.

She looks at him, then away, very frightened.

                        ANGEL (cont'd)
          You don't have to be afraid, you're safe
          here.

                        TINA
          No...

                        ANGEL
          Yes.

But Tina is looking at a crumpled slip of paper on the end
table -- the one Doyle gave Angel: TINA, COFFEE SPOT, S.M.

                        TINA
          Why do you have that?

He looks, she pulls away from him, standing.

                        TINA (cont'd)
          You knew who I was when you walked in there last
          night.

                        ANGEL
          No. I didn't. I just -- had your name, it's complicated.

                        TINA
          I'm sure, big complicated game Russell is working on
          my head. What's he paying you?

                        ANGEL
          He's not, you have to --

                        TINA
          You're just like him!

She shoves him away, grabs a lamp.

                        TINA (cont'd)
          You stay away from me. I'm getting out of here.

                        ANGEL
          Let me...

She hurls the lamp at his head and runs out the back door.

27 INT. ANGEL'S OFFICE LOBBY - DAY

She runs for all she's worth, out of the office. Angel appears, running after her.

> ANGEL
> Tina -- !

Tina runs out of the lobby. Angel close behind. As she hits the SUNLIGHT he grabs her arm.

> ANGEL (cont'd)
> Please listen to --

HIS HAND - on her arm in the sunlight: BURSTS INTO FLAME! She screams. He wrenches his hand back into the shadows, howling in pain and MORPHING into a VAMPIRE. She sees this - runs for her life. He collapses against the building, cradling his hand, breathing hard, watching her go.

28 OMITTED

29 EXT. TINA'S APT. BUILDING - DAY

Not as crummy as Cordelia's but not much better.

30 INT. TINA'S APT. - DAY

She lets herself in, shuts the door. She grabs a small traveling bag, drops it on the open sofa bed, bends down lifts up the mattress, takes out a small .38. She throws a few things in the bag, then sensing a presence, she spins, pointing the gun at: RUSSELL, (late 30's or 40's, charming, incredibly well dressed).

> RUSSELL
> Tina, what are you doing, where have you been? I've been worried sick about you.

> TINA
> What did you do to Denise?

> RUSSELL
> Nothing.

> TINA
> I want the truth, Russell!

> RUSSELL
> She wanted to go home. I bought her a ticket to Pensacola.

> TINA
> No. She's dead.

> RUSSELL
> What do you mean? She called me yesterday, she's trying to get back into school, wanted me to pull strings. Who's been telling you these things?

Tina holds her ground with the gun, looking very shaky.

> RUSSELL (cont'd)
> Look, we both know I live outside the box, but I don't
> go around killing my friends.

He moves towards her, getting very close.

> RUSSELL (cont'd)
> I've had everybody I know looking for you.

She just stares at him, frozen like a deer in the headlights. Tina lets Russell
take the gun out of her hand as:

> RUSSELL (cont'd)
> If you're sick of L.A., if you need rent, you know I
> only want to help you. Just tell me what you want.

> TINA
> (softly)
> I want to go home...

> RUSSELL
> Done. Poor thing...

She lets him put his arms around her.

> RUSSELL (cont'd)
> ...who's been spinning your head like this?

> TINA
> I don't know, I thought you hired him... he turned
> into something...

He strokes her cheek, looks at her compassionately.

> TINA (cont'd)
> ...it was the most horrible thing I've ever seen.

> RUSSELL
> Well, you're young.

And he MORPHS into a HORRIBLE VAMPIRE, much more demon-like than Angel.

Tina opens her mouth but she has nothing left inside with which to scream.
Russell chomps down hard and vicious on her neck.

BLACK OUT.

<u>END OF ACT TWO</u>

<u>ACT THREE</u>

31 INT. TINA'S APT. - DUSK

We HEAR footsteps in the hall outside. The door, left slightly ajar, is pushed
open by Angel.

He sees -- TINA ON THE FLOOR, next to the sofa-bed. He races to her, checks her
pulse. She's long dead. He stops, sees the BLOOD ON HIS OWN HANDS NOW. He stares
at his hand... and suddenly thrusts two fingers in his mouth, tasting the blood,
eyes shut, overwhelmed...

His eyes snap open.

SMASH CUT TO:

32 INT. TINA'S APT. - BATHROOM SINK - DUSK

Angel furiously washing his hands; scrubbing them nearly raw, sickened by what he just did.

He looks in the mirror, which offers no reflection. But he can see, behind him on the floor, Tina's body. A silent witness.

TELEPHONE NEAR TINA - As Angel picks it up, his eyes never leaving her.

INSERT HIS (now clean) hand - as it dials 911.

DISSOLVE TO:

33 INT./EXT. TINA'S APT. NIGHT - LATE

A CORONER studies Tina's body. Two DETECTIVES search for clues, a FINGERPRINT person dusts, etc. CAMERA PULLS BACK, revealing we were looking in the window.

CAMERA CONTINUES BACK to a neighboring rooftop where a shadowy figure stands watch. Angel. He waits, still and silent, as her body is bagged and removed from her home. Then he turns, grim, steps up on the roof ledge, leaps. We see him land on a neighboring roof far below and disappear into the darkness.

DISSOLVE TO:

34 EXT. RUSSELL'S MANSION - DAY

Large iron gates secure the stone wall that surrounds it: a fortress. A GUARD in a KIOSK next to gates keeps watch.

35 INT. RUSSELL'S MANSION - STUDY - DAY

A large, clean space; computers, huge monitors, paintings, empty desk, thick drapes secured against the daylight. Russell lounges near several monitors that track the world's financial markets. But he isn't watching them, he's watching the video Margo shot at her party: footage of Tina. There is a discreet BUZZ on the intercom.

> WILLIAM'S VOICE (O.S.)
> Mr. McDonald from Wolfram and Hart is here, sir.

> RUSSELL
> Show him in, William.

36 INT. RUSSELL'S MANSION - FOYER - DAY

Uniformed maids clean and polish in b.g. WILLIAM the BUTLER shows LINDSEY MCDONALD (smart young lawyer, Wolfram and Hart briefcase in hand) into:

37 INT. RUSSELL'S MANSION - STUDY - DAY

> LINDSEY
> Hello, Mr. Winters. Sorry to disturb you at home.

The Butler bows out, leaving them alone.

                    RUSSELL
          (rewinds, watches Tina on vid again)
          A man is only disturbed to see someone from his
          law firm when he brings bad news. Am I going to be
          disturbed, Lindsey?

                    LINDSEY
          No. The Eitron merger is a go, they caved on
          everything after you... negotiated with their C.F.O.
          We'll bring the final drafts to your office tomorrow.

                    RUSSELL
          Yet you're here today.

Lindsey nods, glances at Tina on screen.

                    RUSSELL (cont'd)
          (re: Tina)
          She had something, didn't she...
          (rewinds again)
          I was sorry to kill her so soon.

Lindsey stares at Tina, then impassively opens his briefcase, shows documents to
Russell.

                    LINDSEY
          Actually you haven't seen her in several weeks. You
          were in conference yesterday with your contract
          lawyers when the unfortunate incident occurred. And
          we've located a witness who's telling the police he
          saw a dark complected man with blood on his hands
          fleeing the scene.

                    RUSSELL
          Impressive.

                    LINDSEY
          Wolfram and Hart is a full service law firm,
          Mr. Winters. It's our job to make our clients' lives
          run more smoothly.

                    RUSSELL
          No ethical dilemmas?

                    LINDSEY
          (smiles politely)
          Very witty, sir.

Lindsey returns papers to briefcase. During the above, the video has continued
playing scenes from the party.

                    RUSSELL
          Who's this?

Lindsey looks to the vid monitor -- shots of Cordelia.

                    RUSSELL (cont'd)
          Fresh face. I'll have to meet her.

Lindsey thoughtfully closes his briefcase, asks:

                         LINDSEY
          Should I alert the firm that this young lady may
          constitute another... long term investment?

                         RUSSELL
          (studies Cor's image)
          I don't think so, I just want something to eat. That
          reminds me...
          (re: market monitor)
          Short Holloman Food Supplies four hundred thousand
          shares.

38 INT. TUNNEL - DAY

Far off, we can hear (and see?) the rumbling subway. This tunnel is dark,
unused, except by the likes of Angel.

He sits by himself, face unreadable. Doyle approaches, slowly.

                         DOYLE
          I heard. I'm sorry.

                         ANGEL
          If I had just... I didn't help her. I failed her.

                         DOYLE
          You're a soldier; you fight. Sometimes you lose.

                         ANGEL
          Maybe the powers that be need to find a better
          soldier... one with a soul worth saving.

                         DOYLE
          You know, they don't consult me with their battle
          plans. But they chose you for a reason.

                         ANGEL
          She was frightened.

                         DOYLE
          Yeah, she panicked! You can't always know what --

                         ANGEL
          No, I mean... her eyes, the way she would look around
          her, like -- just waiting to see what was gonna hit
          her next.

                         DOYLE
          She got to you.

                         ANGEL
          And I was supposed to help her.

                         DOYLE
          I don't know. Maybe she was supposed to help you.
          Maybe she had something to give you.

                         ANGEL
          Like what?

                         DOYLE
          Grief.

Angel looks at him, considering.

                         DOYLE (cont'd)
          There's a particularly nasty vampire out there. Rich,
          protected, can do any damn thing he wants. He's
          killed, and he'll keep on killing till someone's mad
          enough to take him down.

He gets in Angel's face.

                         DOYLE (cont'd)
          What you need, boy, is a bit a' therapy. You have
          great pain. It's time to share it.

SMASH CUT TO:

39 OMITTED

40 INT. STACEY'S GYM SUPPLIES - DAY

As THUG 1 comes crashing through the plate glass window. Angel has Stacey by the
throat, pressed up against the wall.

                         ANGEL
          Where does he live, how much security does he have?

                              STACEY
          Listen hot shot, whatever she was to you, you better
          forget it. You have no idea who you're dealing with
          here.

                              ANGEL
          Russell? Lemme guess: not big on the daylight or the
          mirrors, drinks a lot of V-8?

                              STACEY
          You get in his way, he'll kill you, he'll kill
          everyone you care about.

Angel tightens his grip, Stacey nearly faints.

                              ANGEL
          There's nobody left I care about.

41 INT. CORDELIA'S CRUMMY APT. - DAY

Cordelia, in sweat pants and t, sits cross legged on her bed, breathing slowly
and deeply. Next to her the book: MEDITATION FOR A BOUNTIFUL LIFE.

                              CORDELIA
          I am somebody...
          (breathes)
          I matter...
          (breathes)
          People will be attracted to my positive energy and
          help me achieve my goals...

She glances at phone machine. The message counters registers a big zero. She
breathes again.

                              CORDELIA (cont'd)
          ...I am right where I'm supposed to be and not DYING
          FOR SOMETHING TO EAT!

She hurls the book across the room, sits there on the verge of tears. The phone
RINGS. She jumps, startled, then answers in a "positive" tone of voice.

                              CORDELIA (cont'd)
          Hello, this is Cordelia Chase.

INTERCUT:

MARGO - ON THE PHONE IN HER HIGH-RISE - DAY

                              MARGO
          Cor, it's Margo, you were such a hit at my party.

                              CORDELIA
          Thanks, I had a great time. I want to have you over to
          my place...
          (re: shabby digs)
          ...soon as I'm done redecorating.

                              MARGO
          Well guess who saw my videotape of the party and guess
          who wants to meet you...

                              CORDELIA
            A director? A manager? An assistant to an assistant
            who's ready to spring for lunch?

                              MARGO
            Russell Winters.

                              CORDELIA
            The investment guy?

As the conversation continues, it is INTERCUT with the events that it is leading
up to.

42 EXT. STREETS - NIGHT

Possibly slo mo, a long black limo glides into frame.

                              MARGO (O.S.)
            Oh, Cordelia, he's a lot more than that. He helps
            people get started in their careers, he knows everyone
            and... he wants to meet you tonight.

                              CORDELIA (O.S.)
            Tonight? Well, let me check my calendar...
            (waits a beat)
            ...I'll have to cancel a couple of things but I'm sure
            I can --

43 INT. LIMO - NIGHT

Cordelia rides in plush comfort. She sips a mineral water, munches some nuts.
Hums a little happy tune to herself.

                              CORDELIA (O.S.)
            Wait. I don't have to have sex with him, do I? Cause I
            couldn't... I'm nearly positive that I couldn't --

                              MARGO (O.S.)
            No, no, he just likes to help people. I don't think he
            enjoys sex at all.

44 EXT. RUSSELL'S MANSION - NIGHT

Limo approaches. GUARD in the KIOSK recognizes the car, hits a button. The huge
iron gates swing open.

                              CORDELIA (O.S.)
            Oh good!

                              MARGO (O.S.)
            He'll send a limo for you at eight.

45 INT. LIMO - NIGHT

Cordelia peeks out at the impressive mansion. (Dialogue now is inside the limo,
no longer on the phone.)

                              CORDELIA
            "People will be attracted to my positive energy and
            help me achieve my goals." Oh yeah.

Happily, she pops a nut into her mouth.

46 EXT. RUSSELL'S MANSION - NIGHT

The limo pulls in and up the long drive as the gates swing shut, closing and
locking Cordelia in with a resounding CLANG

BLACK OUT.

END OF ACT THREE

ACT FOUR

47 INT. ANGEL'S APT. - NIGHT

Angel is wrapping up an impressive array of gear: timer, detonators, plastique
explosive, small set of tools, rope, etc. Doyle watches.

> DOYLE
> Wow, you're really going to war here. Guess you've
> seen a few in your time.

> ANGEL
> Fourteen. Not counting Vietnam -- they never declared
> it.

> DOYLE
> Well, this is good, you're taking charge, fighting
> back -- do you really need all this?

> ANGEL
> A Girl Scout told me: be prepared.

> DOYLE
> Well, best of luck. I got some fairly large coin
> riding on the Vikings tonight, but I'll be with you
> in spirit --

> ANGEL
> You're driving.

> DOYLE
> What? But -- no. No no, I'm not combat-ready. I'm just
> the messenger.

> ANGEL
> And I'm the message.

48 EXT. RUSSELL MANSION - NIGHT - ESTABLISHING

49 INT. RUSSELL'S MANSION - NIGHT

The Butler leads Cordelia through the cavernous place. She looks around, taking
it all in, impressed.

50 INT. RUSSELL'S MANSION - STUDY - NIGHT

The Butler shows her in, and Russell rises to greet her.

> RUSSELL
> Hi, I'm Russell. Thank you so much for coming.

39

He waves the Butler away, who exits. Cor turns to Russell, trying to think of conversation.

> CORDELIA
> So, nice place, I love the curtains. Not afraid to emphasize the curtains.

> RUSSELL
> I have old fashioned tastes.

> CORDELIA
> I grew up in a nice home. It wasn't like this but we did have a room or two we didn't even know what they were for.

He smiles.

> CORDELIA (cont'd)
> Then the I.R.S. got all huffy about my folks forgetting to pay taxes for, well, ever. They took it all.

> RUSSELL
> And Margo says you're an actress. That's going well?

> CORDELIA
> Oh, yeah, it's great, I've had a lot of opportunities, the hands in the Liqui-Gel commercial were almost mine by like one or two girls, and... well... it's not everything I...

The facade crumbles. She looks at Russell forlornly, wondering what he will require of her.

51 EXT. RUSSELL'S MANSION - NIGHT

The GUARD in the KIOSK watches the security monitors (that show front, side, back, etc. of the property) . He looks up as Angel's car pulls up, Doyle at the wheel. Angel gets out.

> ANGEL
> Hi, I think we're lost... I'm looking for Cliff Drive -- hey, what ya' watchin'? Is that the Vikings?

Angel leans over, looks at the monitor that shows Angel's car and the front of the house.

ANGEL'S HAND - reaches out, grabs the transmitting wire from the video camera on the gate, rips it out. The monitor goes snowy.

> GUARD
> Hey, what are you --

The Guard fishes for his gun -- Angel knocks him out.

> ANGEL
> (to Doyle)
> Tie him up. I'm out in ten minutes or I'm not coming out.

                         DOYLE
                Ten minutes.

Angel grabs his gear and bolts.

AT THE WALL - ANGEL LEAPS, grabs the top, pulls himself upright and runs along
it into the night.

ANOTHER ANGLE - Angel runs along a section of wall closer to the house. He
stops, crouches low.

ANGEL'S POV - An armed guard walks the property. As the guard rounds a corner --

ANGEL runs on the wall and LEAPS. He lands on the roof of the mansion. He moves
across the roof, jumps again.

THE SIDE YARD - Angel lands, looks for guards, attaches plastique and detonator
to an auxiliary generator. He heads around the corner of the house to THE FUSE
BOX, starts working on it.

52 INT. RUSSELL'S MANSION - STUDY - NIGHT

Cordelia is speaking quietly, opening up to Russell more than she would have
intended.

                              CORDELIA
                I've tried really hard, you know? Usually when I try
                at something I succeed right away. I just thought this
                would be... but I don't know anybody, I don't even
                have any friends out here...

                              RUSSELL
                Now you know me. And you don't have to worry anymore.

                              CORDELIA
                (looking down)
                What do you want me to do?

                              RUSSELL
                Just tell me what you want.

Cordelia tries to collect herself - and to stall the intimacy of the moment.

                              CORDELIA
                Oh, God, I'm sorry -- here I am getting all weepy in
                front of you...
                (looks around for a mirror)
                I probably look really scary - I finally get invited
                to a nice place with no mirrors and lots of curtains
                and hey, you're a vampire.

                              RUSSELL
                (caught off guard)
                What? No I'm not.

                              CORDELIA
                Are too.

                              RUSSELL
                (removes hand)
                I don't know what you're talking about.

                                  CORDELIA
            I'm from Sunnydale, we had our own hellmouth, I know a
            vampire when I...
            (as it sinks in)
            ...am alone with one in his fortress-like home and you
            know I'm just so light-headed from hunger I'm wacky
            and kidding!! Hah hah....
            (tiny, off his look)
            ...hah.

53 EXT. RUSSELL'S MANSION - NIGHT

Angel finishes rigging the second auxiliary generator. HEARS SOMETHING. ANOTHER
GUARD rounds the corner, walks right past the generator where we just saw Angel.
As Guard disappears, Angel's feet drop into frame from above. He drops down,
sets a timing device on the generator for ten seconds.

54 INT. RUSSELL'S MANSION - STUDY - NIGHT

Russell and Cordelia, she's scrambling to stay calm.

                                  CORDELIA
            You know one of my very dearest friends is a vam -- do
            you prefer "night person"?

                                  RUSSELL
            Truth is, I'm happy you know. Means we can skip the
            formalities.

                                  CORDELIA
            (really afraid now) Please...

He GROWLS, MORPHS and lunges. She screams and flees into:

55 INT. RUSSELL'S MANSION - MAIN FOYER - CONTINUOUS

Cordy runs up the stairs but Russell is right behind her, grabs her --

56 EXT. RUSSELL'S MANSION - NIGHT - INSERTS

The three small explosives go off: BAM, BAM, BAM!

57 OMITTED

58 INT. RUSSELL'S MANSION - STUDY - NIGHT

Suddenly dark, except for shafts of moonlight. Russell, in vamp face, looks
around as:

                              ANGEL (O.S.)
            Russell Winters.

He turns as Angel steps out of the shadows.

                                  CORDELIA
             Angel?

                                    RUSSELL
            What do you want?

                         ANGEL
              I have a message from Tina.

Russell blanches slightly at the name.

                         RUSSELL
              You've made a very big mistake, coming here.

                         CORDELIA
              You don't know who he is, do you? Oh boy, are you
              about to get your ass kicked!

Angel and Russell charge each other, trade a couple of quick vicious punches.
Russell knocks Angel back hard enough to make him go to vampface.

                         RUSSELL
              One of us? Didn't you get the owner's manual? We don't
              help them, we eat them!

Angel charges and gets the better of Russell, but Russell holds back Angel's
stake.

The doors burst open and TWO GUARDS run in GUNS DRAWN.

                         RUSSELL (cont'd)
                   (re: Cordelia)
              Kill her.

The Guards point at Cordelia. Angel throws away Russell and catapults in front
of her, taking several bullets, tackling her and sending them both over the back
railing. They hit the floor and bolt for the back door.

59 EXT. RUSSELL'S MANSION - NIGHT - DOYLE

Doyle reacts to more gunshots.

                         DOYLE
              That's it. I'm gone.

Doyle throws car into gear, burns rubber down the
street.

CLOSE - DOYLE BEHIND THE WHEEL - Scared and not
proud of it. He suddenly wrenches the wheel.

                    DOYLE (cont'd)
                   Dammit.

THE CAR - Squeals and turns in a big
180, starts barreling towards the big
metal gates.

DOYLE - lets out a WAR CRY!

                    DOYLE (cont'd)
                   Yaaahhhhhhhh!!!

THE CAR gains tremendous speed and RAMS INTO THE GATES! -- which hold just fine unlike the front bumper and hood of the car which crumple like a cheap toy.

                    DOYLE (cont'd)
             (beat)
             Good gate.

Doyle backs the car -- smoking and lurching but still running -- off the gate as Angel (badly wounded) and Cordelia drop down the last couple of feet from the wall. They get in.

                    DOYLE (cont'd)
             (re: car)
             I had a little...
             (more SHOTS)
             ...we'll talk later.

He hits the gas, they lurch away.

60 INT. ANGEL'S APT. - NIGHT

Angel's shirt is off. Cor is telling Doyle (with forceps) how to remove the bullets from Angel's torso. Angel winces in pain.

                    DOYLE
             Doin' my best, buddy...

                    CORDELIA
             (to Angel)
             We can't actually kill you unless we put a stake
             through your heart, right?

                    ANGEL
             Maybe you should get one.

                    DOYLE
             Got it.

He drops the bullet next to three others they've pulled.

                    CORDELIA
             Finally, thought I was going to faint while barfing.

They bandage Angel's wounded torso as:

                    CORDELIA (cont'd)
             So it's over, right? We're both going to be okay, you
             put the fear of God in that Russell guy, he's not
             gonna come looking for me, right?

Doyle looks at Angel, who is worried about that very thing.

61 EXT. SKYSCRAPER - DAY - ESTABLISHING

A tower o' downtown power. RUSSELL WINTERS ENTERPRISES proclaims the fancy brushed steel sign in front.

62 INT. SKYSCRAPER - CONFERENCE ROOM - DAY

CLOSE ON THE WOLFRAM AND HART BRIEFCASE as Lindsey removes some documents.

                         LINDSEY
          The Eitron mutual trust binder is ready for your
          signature.

Lindsey, speaking to Russell at the far end of the table, hands the docs to a
SMART YOUNG LAWYERESS on his right who hands it down the line of smart YOUNG
LAWYERS to Russell.

                         LINDSEY (cont'd)
          Also, we spoke to our office in Washington this
          morning, the new tax law we lobbied will knock three
          percent off gross taxes and kick up profits accordingly.
          We were pretty pleased with that down at the firm.
               (more papers)
          As to the intruder who broke into your home last
          night, the local authorities have no information on
          him but we have several top private investigators --

The door is kicked open and Angel, looking a little ragged, still smarting from
his wounds, walks in.

                         LINDSEY (cont'd)
          -- looking into his whereabouts.

                         RUSSELL
          I believe we've located him.

Lindsey moves to Angel, hands him his card.

                         LINDSEY
          I'm with Wolfram and Hart. Mr. Winters has never been
          accused of and shall never be convicted of any crime.
          Ever. Should you continue to harass our client, we
          shall be forced to bring you into the light of day --
          a place, I'm told, that's not all that healthy for you.

Lindsey smiles. Angel looks down at the lawyer's card in his hand, then at
Russell in his comfy executive chair.

                         RUSSELL
          Angel, we do things a certain way in L.A.

                         ANGEL
          Well, I'm new here.

                         RUSSELL
          But you're a civilized man. We don't have to go
          attacking each other. Look at me. I pay my taxes, keep
          my name out of the paper; I don't make waves. And in
          return I can do pretty much anything I want.

                         ANGEL
          Really?

Angel lifts his foot, rests it on the chair between Russell's legs --

                         ANGEL (cont'd)
          Can you fly?

-- and KICKS with all his might...   45

RUSSELL AND HIS CHAIR - rocket back fast -- crashing into and through the wall of glass behind him.

63 EXT. SKYSCRAPER - DAY

The glass breaks, Russell and his chair come flying out into the sunlight. As he falls, screaming bloody murder, he bursts into flame and burns to vampire dust.

64 INT. SKYSCRAPER - CONFERENCE ROOM - DAY

Angel, just out of the direct sunlight flooding in through the broken window, stands watching, the array of stone-faced lawyers behind him.

                    ANGEL
          Guess not.

Angel turns and goes. A moment, then Lindsey speed-dials his phone.

                    LINDSEY
          (into phone)
          Set an interoffice meeting for 4 o'clock. It seems we
          have a new player in town.
          (listens)
          No, no need to disturb the senior partners with this.
          Not yet.

He snaps his briefcase shut. The others follow suit, calm and cool. As they file out --

65 EXT. SKYSCRAPER - DAY

Looking at the RUSSELL WINTERS ENTERPRISES sign as Russell's chair smashes into the ground and bounces, a few dusty ashes sprinkling down in its wake.

66 EXT. ANGEL'S BUILDING - DAY - ESTABLISHING

67 INT. ANGEL'S APT. - DAY

Angel sits by himself, by the phone. A moment, and he picks it up, dials. Waits.

                    BUFFY'S VOICE
          Hello? Hello?

He hangs up. Doyle enters from upstairs.

                    DOYLE
          What happened with Russell?

                    ANGEL
          He went into the light.

                    DOYLE
          Yet ya' don't seem in a celebratin' mood.

                    ANGEL
          I killed a vampire. I didn't help anyone.

                              DOYLE
                    You sure a' that?

                              CORDELIA (O.S.)
                    AAGHHLL!

The boys bolt upstairs.

68 INT. ANGEL'S OFFICE - DAY

They come up to find: The old desks and file cabinets have been dusted and moved
into the inner and outer office spaces. Cordelia, wearing one of Angel's shirts,
sleeves rolled up, has been dusting and shoving furniture around.

                              CORDELIA
                    Cockroach. In the corner. I'd say a bantamweight.

Doyle goes to check. Cordy turns to Angel.

                              CORDELIA (cont'd)
                    Okay, first thing, we have to call an exterminator.
                    And a sign painter, we should have a name on the door.

                              ANGEL
                    Okay, I'm confused... again...

                              CORDELIA
                    Oh, Doyle told me about your little mission and all
                    and I was saying, if we're gonna help people out,
                    maybe a small charge, a fee, you know, something to
                    help pay the rent, and my salary... You need someone
                    to organize things, and you're not exactly rolling in
                    it, Mr. I-was-alive-for-two-hundred-years-and-never-
                    developed-an-investment-portfolio.

                              ANGEL
                    You want to charge people?

                              CORDELIA
                    Not everybody. But sooner or later you'll have to help
                    some rich people, right?
                    (to Doyle)
                    Right?

                              DOYLE
                    Possibly.

                              CORDELIA
                    Hand me that box. So I figure we'll charge based on a
                    case by case analysis, but with me working for a flat
                    fee.

Angel regards her a moment, taking all this in. For a moment, her bravado slips,
and she looks at him meekly.

                              CORDELIA (cont'd)
                    I mean, that is... if you think you could use me...

A beat, and Angel hands her the box, smiling kindly at her. She takes it happily
and exits to the outer office, calling back:

                    CORDELIA (cont'd)
          Of course this is just temporary, till my inevitable
          stardom takes effect.

                    DOYLE
          You made a good choice. She'll provide a connection to
          the world. She has a very humanizing influence.

                    ANGEL
          You think she's a hottie.

                    DOYLE
          Oh, she's a stiffener, can't lie about that. But she
          could use a hand.

                    ANGEL
          True.

                    DOYLE
          There's a lot of people in this city need helpin'.

                    ANGEL
          So I noticed.

                    DOYLE
          You game?

The camera pushes in on Angel, as a small smile creeps onto his face.

69 EXT. ROOFTOP - NIGHT

He stands in his long coat near the edge of a tall downtown rooftop: part
gargoyle, part Guardian Angel; the whole of L.A. laid out before him, keeping
watch over his city.. .

                    ANGEL (V.O.)
          I'm game.

BLACK OUT.

                    THE END

Executive Producers
JOSS WHEDON & DAVID GREENWALT

Co-Producer
SKIP SCHOOLNIK

Associate Producer
R.D. PRICE

Co-Starring
JON INGRASSIA As Stacy
RENEE RIDGELEY As Margo
SAM PANCAKE As Manager
JOSH HOLLOWAY As Good Looking Guy
GINA McCLAIN As Janice

Director of Photography
HERB DAVIS

Production Designer
CAREY MEYER

Edited By
REGIS B. KIMBLE

Unit Production Manger
KELLY A. MANNERS

First Assistant Director
IAN WOOLF

Second Assistant Director
ROBERT PAPAZIAN, JR.

Score By
CHRISTOPHE BECK

Main Theme By
HOLLY KNIGHT
CAMI ELEN
JYMM THOMAS

Performed By
DARLING VIOLETTA

Casting By AMY McINTYRE   BRITT ANYA COLOFF   JENNIFER FISHMAN
Costume Designer JESSICA PAZDERNIK
Art Director WILLIAM V. RYDER
Set Designer WILL BATTS
Set Decorator SANDY STRUTH
Leadman CHRIS CARRIVEAU
Construction Coordinator BRUCE DI VALERIC
Property Master COURTNEY JACKSON
Production Sound Mixer BEAU BAKER
Chief Lighting Technician RICK WEST
Key Grip MATT MANIA
Camera Operator GUY SKINNER
Special Effects Coordinator MIKE GASPAR
Script Supervisor JAIN SEKULAR
Location Manager MITCHELL BINDER
Stunt Coordinator JEFF CADIENTE
Make-up Supervisor DAYNE JOHNSON
Head Hair Stylist DIANA ACREY
Make-up Effects DAVE MILLER
Transportation Coordinator ROBERT ELLIS
Casting Associate LONNIE HAMERMAN
Production Auditor EDWIN L. PEREZ
Production Supervisor MARC D. ALPERT
ANGEL - "CITY OF" - EPS, #1ADH01
Production Coordinator ELYSE RAMSDELL
Script Coordinator MEREDYTH SMITH
Assistant to David Greenwalt JESSE STERN
Assistant to Joss Whedon DIEGO GUTIERREZ
Assistant to Howard Gordon JOSE MOLINA
Assistant to Kelly A. Manners DAVID BURNS
Post Production Coordinator JENNIFER DAVIS
Assistant Editor MARK GOLDMAN
Post Production Sound Provided by TODD A STUDIOS WEST
Supervising Sound Editor ROBERT EWING
Re-Recording ADAM SAWELSON   KURT KASSULKE   RON EVANS
Music Editor FERNAND BOS
Music Coordinator JOHN KING
Post Production Services And Visual Effects by DIGITAL MAGIC
Visual Effects Supervisor LONI PERISTERE
Main Title Design By REGIS B. KIMBLE
Processing By DELUXE

ANGEL

issue two   scriptbook ™

Episode
A HOLE IN THE WORLD

Written By
JOSS WHEDON

ANGEL™

"A HOLE IN THE WORLD"

WRITTEN BY

JOSS WHEDON

Starring:
DAVID BOREANAZ
ALEXIS DENISOF
J. AUGUST RICHARDS
AMY ACKER
ANDY HALLETT
JAMES MARSTERS

Created By
JOSS WHEDON
&
DAVID GREENWALT

Guest Starring:
JENNIFER GRIFFIN
JONATHAN M. WOODWARD
SARAH THOMPSON

Written and Directed By
JOSS WHEDON

JOSS WHEDON

ANGEL™

"A HOLE IN THE WORLD"

WRITTEN BY

JOSS WHEDON

JOSS WHEDON IN

1 EXT. BURKLE HOME - DAY
(SOME EIGHT YEARS BACK)

It's rural suburban, very pleasant but a little run down. A nice place on a nice day in a nice neighborhood.

                              ROGER (O.S.)
               I just don't see why.

2 INT. BURKLE HOUSEHOLD - FRED'S ROOM - CONTINUING

FRED is in her room, packing for grad school. The room is small, and decorated in a mostly typical way, except for the physics genius accoutrement.

Her parents are with her, TRISH handing her things, ROGER by the door.

                              ROGER
               I don't see why it has to be this way.

                              TRISH
               Oh hush. He was doing this in bed all last night.
               Kept the dogs up.

                              ROGER
               There's plenty of good schools in the area.

                              FRED
               I know. And I have a nice room, and could meet a
               nice boy, and we could get married and live in my
               nice room - -

                              TRISH
               He would have to be a smallish fellah --

                              FRED
               -- And have sweet little babies that can sleep in
               the drawer.

                              ROGER
               I do not see a downside to this plan.

                              FRED
               Daddy, I love you like pancakes. But I'm gettin' the
               hell out of here.

                              TRISH
               Language...

                              ROGER
               She should say it! That' s where she's going: Hell-A.

                              FRED
               It's "Los Angeles". The City of Angels, remember?

                              ROGER
               You meet one Angel there, I'll eat the dogs. Bunch
               a junkies and spoilt movie actors, that's who you're
               gonna meet.

                    FRED
        In the physics graduate program at UCLA.

                    ROGER
        You don't know...

                    TRISH
        Sweetie, why don't you check the Chevy one more time.
        I don't wanna be worrying about her getting there when
        I'm supposed to be worrying about her being there. It
        muddles things.

                    ROGER
        Chevy's fine.
        (starts to go, turns)
        And I slept in a drawer till I was three, didn't stunt
        me none.

He's gone. Fred continues packing.

                    FRED
        Did you call Bethany, is it okay --

                    TRISH
        Late as you like, she says she'll leave you a key if
        they turn in.

                    FRED
        I know I forgot something.

                    TRISH
        Well you just call us up and we can drive it up to you
        and move in, no problem.

                    FRED
        Mom...

                    TRISH
        I'm just scaring you --

                    FRED
        I'm gonna miss you both just as hard.

                    TRISH
        (gently smiling)
        No.

                    FRED
        Of course I am!

                    TRISH
        Not half of half as hard. You have a child someday,
        you'll know what I mean.

                    FRED
        I'll call you lots.

                    TRISH
        I know you will.

Huggage. Fred pulls away.

                    FRED
Feigenbaum! She grabs a tattered, handmade doll from
a shelf, puts it in the suitcase. Can't make the trip
without Feigenbaum.

                    TRISH
He doesn't quite look up to it...

                    FRED
Hush. He's the master of chaos, he'll love L.A. All my
junkie movie actor friends...

                    TRISH
Don't you joke. You gotta promise me you're gonna be
careful.

                    FRED
I'm gonna study, mom. I'm gonna learn every damn thing
they know up there, and figure out some stuff they
don't. And I'll be careful. I'll even be dull. Boring.
Cross my heart.

3 INT. BASEMENT - NIGHT

(PRESENT DAY)

Fred is screaming as she wields a flamethrower, arcing the roar of fire right over camera.

WIDEN to see she's in a sewer, roasting a bunch of large creature eggs.

A creature starts to burst out of an unburned egg -- and is promptly shotgunned into chunks.

ANGLE ON WES recocking the shotgun, moving toward Fred, who turns off the flame.

> FRED
> I think we got the nest.

> WESLEY
> The others are finishing the sweep. Nasty little buggers.

> FRED
> They're kind of cool, physiologically. They reproduce by vomiting up crystals that attract and mutate the microbes around them to form eggs.

> WESLEY
> Are you **trying** to turn me on?

She smiles.

> FRED
> It is kind of romantic. A roaring fire, snug little nest...

> WESLEY
> (holding up a flask)
> A warm twelve year old single malt...

> FRED
> Ooh!

She swigs. Looks at Wes, and they come closer -- shotgun and flamethrower kind of getting in the way there for a sec -- then kiss, framed by the fire behind them. After.. .

> FRED (cont'd)
> You know... someday very soon I'm bringing you to my apartment and...

> WESLEY
> If you even finish that sentence I won't sleep a wink tonight.

> FRED
> Well... soon. When I'm a little less covered in gasoline.

                              WESLEY
               Soon.

They kiss again, until --

                              SPIKE (O.S.)
               I don't see what the bloody fuss is all about!

                              ANGEL (O.S.)
               The fuss? The FUSS?

                              SPIKE
               (entering)
               The thing was on your back! It was about to strike,
               what was I supposed to do?

Angel enters as well. He has a sword though him, hilt in his solarplexus, blade
out the back with a giant nasty-bug also impaled on it.

                              ANGEL
               Ask me to turn around?

                              SPIKE
               Heat of battle. Didn't have time.

                              ANGEL
               You just like stabbing me.

                              SPIKE
               I'm shocked -- shocked! -- that you would think that.
               I much prefer hitting you with blunt instruments.

                              ANGEL
               You know, we only invited you along cause we felt
               sorry for you.

                              SPIKE
               Weren't for me you'd be bugfood so quit whinging.

                              FRED
               Angel?

                              ANGEL
               I'll be all right --

                              FRED
               No, I just want the bug. It's in good shape and I'd
               like to take it back to the lab.
               (to Wes)
               Always like a new specimen...

4 INT. WOLFRAM & HART - LAB - NIGHT

The doors slam open as a huge sarcophagus is wheeled in on a sort of gurney by
an equally huge WORKMAN.

KNOX is working, looks up in surprise.

                              KNOX
                Whoah, hello, what is this?

                              MAN
                Delivery.

                              KNOX
                Ancient relics is two floors down.

                              MAN
                Invoice reads Science Department. Winifred Burkle.

                              KNOX
                Well, do I have to sign...

                              MAN
                Been signed.

And he's gone. Knox looks confused, then looks closely at the sarcophagus.

It's intricately carved, with signs and runes and big damn jewels. He moves
closer to it, fascinated...

                              KNOX
                Winifred Burkle. Beauty, brains, and a big, scary-
                looking coffin thing. Some people just have it all...

He moves away. As we push in on it...

BLACK OUT.

                         END OF TEASER

                            ACT ONE

5 EXT. WOLFRAM AND HART - DAY

To establish.

6 INT. WOLFRAM & HART - GUNN'S OFFICE - DAY

GUNN is moving about the office, pulling something from the
fax and merrily singing (as Wesley approaches from the hall)

                              GUNN
                THREE LITTLE MAIDS WHO ALL UNWARY/
                COME FROM A LADIES' SEMINARY/
                FREED FROM ITS GENIUS TUTELARY/
                THREE LITTLE MAIDS FROM SCHOOL/
                THREE LITTLE **MAI**...
                (sees Wes)
                AND YOU DON'T STOP... WITH ALL THE
                LADIES AND THE BUTT AND **OH**-OH AND...
                GANGSTA... BUTT... What's up?

                              WESLEY
                I should ask you. You seem unutterably cheery.

                              GUNN
                I am, I am. Look, I gotta be straight with you 'cause
                this is kind of blowing my mind.

                        WESLEY
          Tell me.

                        GUNN
          Fred and I are getting back together.

Wesley can't speak.

                        GUNN (cont'd)
          She was so keyed up from last night's fight she asked
          me over, we ended up talking to each other for hours,
          like old times and then all of a sud- I can't even
          keep this up 'cause your face is gonna make me **weep**.
          Wes, I'm SO messing with you.

                        WESLEY
          I, oh, no I... next time you really should... die.

                        GUNN
          Come on! Brother gets a dig in, that's my right.

                        WESLEY
          So you know that - -

                        GUNN
          It's on every Blackberry in the building. No secrets
          in the House of Pain.

                        WESLEY
          And... is it all right? With you... Fred and me...

                        GUNN
          Last year you wouldn't've asked me that question. The
          man becomes civilized.
          (thinks a beat)
          It's a little weird, which I didn't expect. Not
          a lot of women like Fred. But I'm cool. Our
          thing is long done and I know how you feel
          about her.

                        WESLEY
          Thank you.

                        GUNN
          And to add the necessary boilerplate -- You ever hurt
          her, I'm a kill you like a chicken.

                        WESLEY
          Acceptable terms.

                        LORNE
          (entering)
          Hey Romeo, can I bump ya? I need a word with M.C.
          Yum-Yum here.

                        GUNN
          How'd you hear me --

                              LORNE
            Vent leads right to the breakroom. The girls from the
            steno are puttin' in a request for a medley from
            "Princess Ida" but what I need is to talk residuals
            and merchandising.

                              GUNN
            For what?

                              LORNE
            When Angel got turned into a puppet and went on that
            kids show and, you know, killed that other puppet...
            bigger than Pokemon. There's gonna be dolls and
            playsets and we don't wanna let this slip away.

                              GUNN
            I think we got tastier fish to fry.

                              WESLEY
            Yes, you said something was up before you made that
            tasteless and horrible joke at my expense.

                              GUNN
            Lindsey McDonald.

                              WESLEY
            You know where he is?

                              GUNN
            Settle for "was"? He can hide from the Senior Partners
            but not from the DWP and not from my many, many ears.

He hands Wes a piece of paper.

                              WESLEY
            He was living here?

                              GUNN
            Under the name "Doyle." Way he was messing with Angel
            and Spike, could be he had some other schemes laid
            out. And the Senior Partners took him out fast. I
            don't think he had time to pack.

                              WESLEY
            Worth checking out --

                              LORNE
            How is this better than fluffy Angel doll rights?

                              WESLEY
            Nice work. You should tell Angel.

                              GUNN
            You can tell him.
            (beat)
            I ain't going in there.

They look over at Angel's office. Shouting voices can just be heard, those of
Angel and Spike. The boys listen, grimacing.

> WESLEY
> And what is it now?

7 INT. WOLFRAM & HART - ANGEL'S OFFICE - DAY

Angel and Spike are in the thick of it, pacing about the conference table.

> SPIKE
> It's bollocks, Angel. It's your brand of bollocks from
> first to last.

> ANGEL
> You can't ever see the big picture, can you? You can't
> see **any** picture.

> SPIKE
> I'm talking about something primal. Savagery. Brutal,
> animal instinct.

> ANGEL
> And that wins out every time with you. The human race
> has **evolved,** Spike.

> SPIKE
> Into a bunch of mamby-pamby self-analyzing wankers
> that could never hope to overcome pure aggressors --

> ANGEL
> (on "never")
> We're smarter -- and we're bigger! Plus there's
> a thing called teamwork, not to mention the
> superstitious terror of your "pure aggressors" --

> SPIKE
> (overlapping)
> You just want it to be the way you --

> ANGEL
> It's not about what I **want**!

> WESLEY
> Sorry. Is this something we should all be discussing?

They stop, seeing he has entered.

> ANGEL
> No.

> WESLEY
> It just sounds a little serious.

> ANGEL
> It was mostly... theoretical, we --

> SPIKE
> We were working out a...
> (laying it out)
> If cavemen and astronauts got into a fight, who would win?
> (Loong beat)
> Ah.
> (Smaller beat)

                         WESLEY (cont'd)
            You've been yelling at each other for forty minutes
            about this?

No reply.

            Do the astronauts have weapons?

                         SPIKE/ANGEL
            No.

8 INT. WOLFRAM & HART - LAB - DAY

Fred is looking over the sarcophagus.

                         FRED
            It is beautiful, sort of.

                         KNOX
            I couldn't find any invoice for it. I thought maybe
            you went crazy on E-Bay.

                         FRED
            No, no E-Bay. After the commemorative plate incident,
            I'm living clean. Did you run a spectral analysis?

                         KNOX
            Everything's bouncing off it. Which doesn't thrill me.

                         FRED
            Yeah, let's not be hasty about opening it. Probably
            just a mummy, but...

                         KNOX
            Mummies can be a lot more trouble, than you'd think.
            And you're seeing Wesley now.

                         FRED (
            thrown)
            Un, oh. Okay. That's not connected to mummies in some
            way...

                         KNOX
            No, I just wanted to get it out there... I want you
            to know I'm totally good with it. I know I made...
            advances...

                         FRED
            I'm sorry --

                         KNOX
            No, no! The concept of "out of my league" is not
            unknown to me.

                         FRED
            It's not about leagues.

                         KNOX
            Well, I just hope I didn't make you uncomfortable.
            'Cause I love working with you. And that's plenty
            for me.

                              FRED
              You're sweet.

                              KNOX
              You want me to get our hazmats on this baby?

Fred examines it closely.

                              FRED
              Yeah.
              (as he exits)
              And see about where it came from...

She furrows her brow, looking closer. Slowly, almost involuntarily, she moves
her hand toward a jewel in the center.

She touches it, and a spiraled sort of 'mouth' opens, a bit of air blowing at
Fred. She moves back, startled, coughs once as the mouth recloses.

                              KNOX
              (re-entering)
              What happened?

                              FRED
              I don't know! It opened... there was air...

                              KNOX
              Are you okay?

                              FRED
              I think so... That was odd.

                              KNOX
              If you breathed anything in there, you should get
              checked out right now.

                              FRED
              Yeah, I guess. It didn't smell bad...

                              KNOX
              Better safe. I'll get the boys to suit up and work
              this thing over. You scoot over to medical and get
              tested. I don't want you going down with mummy fever.

                              FRED
              Thanks. And Knox?
              (he turns to her)
              Thanks.

8 INT. WOLFRAM & HART - ANGEL'S OFFICE - DAY

Angel sits at his desk. Spike enters.

                              SPIKE
              Harmony pulled me out of a very promising game of
              poker down in accounts receivable, so this better be
              good -- oh, and all of the guys down there agree that
              astronauts don't stand a chance against cavemen, so
              don't even start.

                              ANGEL
              Look. I can't do this any more.

                    SPIKE
Admitting defeat, are you?

                    ANGEL
You and me. It isn't working out.

                    SPIKE

Are you saying we should start annoying other people?

                    ANGEL
I'm saying you should go.

                    SPIKE
Really can't stand the competition, can you?

                    ANGEL
(bridling)
That isn't the --
(chills)
The way I figure it, Lindsey brought you back as a
spirit bound to this place so you'd become invested
in it. He only made you corporeal once you'd gotten
used to it. Attached to it.

                    SPIKE
I'm not attached. I just don't have anywhere else to
go.

                    ANGEL
What if you did?
(off Spike's look)
Wolfram and Hart has offices in every major city in
the world, and a lot more out of it.

                    SPIKE
And I'd what, sit behind a desk all day while everyone
plotted my death? Not in this eternity.

                    ANGEL
Then work the streets. I'll give you the resources
you need to go anywhere: cars, gadgets, expense
account -- you fight the good fight. But in style.
And if possible, in Outer Mongolia.

                    SPIKE
Roving agent. Sort of a Double-Oh-Seven without the
poncy tux. Go anywhere I want.

                    ANGEL
Anywhere. Everywhere.

                    SPIKE
Always did love Tuscany this time of year. How does
that strike you? Buffy looks up from her Cinzano to
see me stepping out of the old Aston Martin. That's an
entrance might be worth the making.

                    ANGEL
So you'll consider my offer.

                         SPIKE
            Hell with that. It's taken.
            (exiting)
            I want it in writing, though. I don't trust you
            corporate types. And I don't wanna end up at some
            youth hostel in Brugenstag 'cause my charge-card
            dried up.

                         ANGEL
            (quiet contempt)
            Bon voyage.

10 INT. WOLFRAM & HART - UPSTAIRS/LOBBY - DAY

Lome and Fred are walking together towards the stairs.

                         FRED
            But that doesn't make any sense.

                         LORNE
            I call it like I see it.

                         FRED
            But the cavemen have fire, that's what they live with
            in their caves! So the Astronauts should at least have
            some kind of weapon...

She stops just at the top of the stairs, smiling at something.

                         FRED (cont'd)
            Hey there.

REVERSE ON WES, just coming up, smiling as well.

                         WESLEY
            Hello. I was on my way to thinking of an excuse to
            come and see you.

                         FRED
            How's it working out?

                         WESLEY

            Really great. Where are you coming from?

                         FRED
            Medical. I breathed some old mummy dust, hadda make
            sure I didn't discover any new germs.

                         WESLEY
            And you're all right?

                         FRED
            They shooed me right off. Mummy-free.

                         WESLEY
            I was hoping to take you out tomorrow night, and I
            don't feature you wrapped in bandages.

                         FRED
            Take me out where?

                    WESLEY
          Can it be a secret?

                    LORNE
          (elbowing past)
          Sheesh! Get a balcony, you two.

                    FRED
          (to Lorne)
          You'll still find me for lunch
          though, right?

                    LORNE
          I'll just look where the sun
          shines.
          (sings)
          YOU ARE MY SUNSHINE, MY ONLY
          SUNSHINE...

                    FRED
          (quietly, to Wes)
          YOU MAKE ME HAPPY...

Lorne's head whips back in desperate alarm. Fred
coughs blood all over Wesley's face.

She pitches down the stairs, Lorne just there to
catch her, Wesley grabbing her as she convulses --

                    WESLEY
          Get medical! **Someone get
          medical now**!

BLACK OUT.

                    END OF ACT ONE

                    ACT TWO

11 INT. HOSPITAL ROOM - DAY

Fred opens her eyes, looking pale and sweaty. She sees Wes, Gunn, Angel, Spike,
Lorne and Knox all gathered round her.

                    FRED
          It's my boys... haven't had this many big, strapping
          men at my bedside since that night with the Varsity
          LaCrosse team...
          (They all look a tad uncomfortable.)
           That was a joke. Not my best joke ever, but y'all
          look like you're gonna poo, so somebody better give
          me a prognosis.

                    WESLEY
          How do you feel?

                    FRED
          Trampled.

LORNE
You gave us all a big scare, Freddies.

ANGEL
You just need to rest. Lab's doing a little bloodwork.

FRED
I'm a mummy, aren't I?

SPIKE
I've fought plenty of mummies and none of them were as
pretty as you. Almost none.

FRED
Now y'all are being too comforting. What's really up?

GUNN
You're sick, and you're making it worse by worrying.

KNOX
We've got that sarcophagus under the scope. If it
gave you anything we'll isolate it in a few hours.

FRED
So you don't know what it is.

ANGEL
Yet.

FRED
Okay.

ANGEL
We're gonna work this. You need anything, you holler.
Shouldn't be long.

FRED
Handsome man saves me.

ANGEL
(smiles)
That's how it works...
(to the guys)
Let's get cracking.

The guys disperse, Gunn running his hand over hers. Wes stays behind.

FRED
"Get cracking". He's such an old fogey.

WESLEY
Are you comfortable?

FRED
I'll be okay.

WESLEY
Yes, you will. I've made reservations and I've no
intention of cancelling them.

FRED
I know you have to go be bookman.

                              WESLEY
                    Yes, this is a job for...
                    (points to a phone)
                    But just hit that line and I'll be here in a
                    heartbeat.

                              FRED
                    Assuming I still have one.

                              WESLEY
                    Hush.

He kisses her forehead.

Angel and Spike have remained, are a distance away.

                              ANGEL
                    Wes and Fred?

                              SPIKE
                    You didn't know?

He watches them a moment.

                              ANGEL
                    I didn't know.

They head out.

12 INT. WOLFRAM & HART - LOBBY - DAY

Wes joins the boys and they all make their way down from the infirmary to the
center of the lobby as they talk:

                              ANGEL
                    How is she taking it?

                              WESLEY
                    She's smarter than all of us put together. She knows
                    it's bad.

                              GUNN
                    How bad? What do we know?

                              KNOX
                    Whatever she's got, it doesn't match up with any of
                    the pathogens in our archive. It's mystical and it's
                    not ours.

                              ANGEL
                    What about the sarcophagus?

                              WESLEY
                    My team is cross checking the symbols but it's also
                    new territory for us.

                              GUNN
                    Angel, what exactly is happening to her. You talked to
                    the doc --

                              WESLEY
                    They have something?

ANGEL
Yeah, I... some parasitic agent is working its way --
I mean as near as they can tell --

WESLEY
(as they land)
Get to the point.

ANGEL
Her organs are cooking. In a day's time they'll liquefy.

They take this in.

SPIKE
No. Not this girl. Not this day.

ANGEL
Wes, you've gotta find out what was in that box. I
need a name, a history --

KNOX
We can't get it open. Not even the lasers --

WESLEY
Where did it come from?

KNOX
Showed up. No return address and I didn't recognize
the guy who brought it. In, now that I think of it,
the middle of the night.

ANGEL
This was deliberate.

LORNE
Senior Partners?

GUNN
Doesn't add up, but I'll hit the white room, talk to
the conduit.

ANGEL
If the partners didn't do this, you gotta get them to
help us.

GUNN
Any way I can.

SPIKE
What about Doyle -- ah, Lindsey? Man loves to play his
games...

ANGEL
I was looking to work the streets, and we've got his
address. For all we know he's sitting there laughing.
(to Spike) If there's muscle work --

SPIKE
Let's make it twice as fast.

                              LORNE
                    (points to himself)
          And baby makes three. In case anybody feels like
          singing.

                              ANGEL
          Good. Guys --

                              WESLEY
          You don't have to say it.

                              ANGEL
          I'll say it anyway.
                    (looks at them)
          Winifred Burkle. Go.

They all split up.

13 INT. HOSPITAL ROOM - DAY

Fred lies there, breathing heavily. Fighting the pain.

14 INT. WOLFRAM & HART - WESLEY'S OFFICE - DAY

A text magically appears on a book. Widen to see Wes looking at it, flipping
pages...

A few of his team are in the room as well, moving about, working...

A LAWYER pokes his head in.

                              LAWYER
          I'm sorry to interrupt, I just need to know if the
          Holbein Clan history was here, it was supposed to be
          faxed to my office...

                              WESLEY
          It can wait.

                              LAWYER
          These guys are really important, I just need the... I
          mean the whole company can't be working Ms. Burkle's
          case.

                              WESLEY
          Of course.

He pulls a .45 from his desk drawer and shoots out one of the Lawyer's knees
without ever looking at him. SCREAMING, the guy drops. Wes's receptionist looks
in, shocked.

                              WESLEY (cont'd)
          Jennifer. Please send anyone else who isn't working
          Ms. Burkle's case to me.

His eyes always on the book.

15 INT. WOLFRAM & HART - WHITE ROOM - DAY

Gunn is alone. He looks about him...

                    GUNN
          Hello? Here kitty kitty... I know there's
          someone in here and it ain't just me.
          (nothing)
          I got important business here. The most important. I'm
          not going anywhere till --

A fist SLAMS into his jaw, sends him hard to the ground. He looks up at the
creature that hit him, quiet surprise on his face.

                    GUNN (cont'd)
          Well what do you know? It is just me.

REVERSE ON GUNN. No cat, no little girl, it's our boy himself, dressed the same,
every inch the same save the glowering intensity of his pitiless gaze.

                    GUNN 2
          You don't wanna be here.

                    GUNN
          I never wanna be here. What happened to the cat?

                    GUNN 2
          The physical form of the conduit is determined by the
          viewer.

                    GUNN
          (rising)
          So I'm looking at me because, what, we're gonna play a
          mirror game? Get our mime on?

> GUNN 2
> You are failing.

> GUNN
> I'm not the issue here.

> GUNN 2
> I believe that you think that.

> GUNN
> You can't let this happen to Fred.

> GUNN 2
> This is the part where I need to be clear.

He flatheels Gunn's chest, sends him into the wall extremely painfully. Advances on him, a little Preacher creeping into his voice.

> GUNN 2 (cont'd)
> I'm not your flunky. I'm not your friend. I am your conduit to the Senior Partners and they are tired of your insolence. Oh yeah, they are not **here** for your **convenience**. If you want Winifred Burkle to live through the night you solve the problem yourself.

> GUNN
> I didn't come for a favor. We can make a deal.

> GUNN 2
> (disdainfully)
> Deals are for the devil.

> GUNN
> You want someone else? A life for hers. You'll get it. You can have mine.

> GUNN 2
> I already do.

He slams Gunn down out of frame. A beat, and he hits him again.

WHITE OUT.

16 INT. LINDSEY'S BEDROOM - DAY

We pull away from the door as we hear the front door crashing open.

> ANGEL (O.S.)
> Figured Lindsey's newfound strength had demon in it.

> SPIKE (O.S.)
> So we can just walk in. Nice.

> LORNE (O.S.)
> Kitchen's an unholy mess.

> ANGEL (O.S.)
> Check everything.

He passes by the door way. Stops, comes back. Stares.

ANGEL

Well I'll be damned all over again.

Swing round to see Eve, sitting on the bed in what must be
one of Lindsey's shirts, looking about as messy as the
bedroom, and righteously freaked.

EVE

Don't touch me!

He enters, as do the others. Lorne moves to one side, to let the two vamps
approach the bed.

ANGEL

Hiding out from the Senior Partners, Eve? How many
sick days do you get before they dock you?

EVE

What do you want?

ANGEL

Fred's dying. Some mystical parasite. Ring a bell?

EVE

I don't know what you're talking about.

SPIKE

What about your boyfriend, luv? He have some wacky
scheme brewing? Sending coffins about?

EVE

You two stay away from me.

ANGEL

Look, Eve, this happens quickly or very, very slowly.

SPIKE

Sarcophagus. Older than anything we know.

EVE

Lindsey and I had nothing to do with that. I'm not
lying -- I'm not.
(looks around)
Have you... heard from him? About him?

SPIKE

Oh, this is truly poetical.

ANGEL

You're not saying what we need to hear.

EVE

(standing)
Why would we do anything to Fred? Why would we even
care about her?

Lorne punches her in the face, sends her back onto the bed
As she sits up, blood on her lip...

                    LORNE
          Ow! Hey, sorry, that was a knuckle buster! I'm Jake
          LaMotta over here, it's pathetic!
          (leaning into her)
          Here's the thing, Eve. You're gonna sing for me, and
          I'm gonna read you. Right now. And here's one more
          thing -- Winifred Burkle once told me, after a sinful
          amount of Chinese food and in lieu of absolutely
          nothing, she said "I think a lot of people would be
          green if they could. Your shade. If they had the
          choice." If I hear one note, one quarter-note that
          tells me you were involved in this these two won't
          have time to kill you. Anything by Diane Warren will
          also result in your death. Except "Rhythm of the
          Night".

                    EVE
          I wanna help, I swear to you. I've got nothing against
          Fred --

                    ANGEL
          Say it with a song in your heart.

She looks at all of them, awkwardly. . .

                    EVE
          (song Lindsey sang in Caritas)Pretty as a picture,
          she is like a golden ring. Settles me with love and
          laughter, I can't feel a thing.

Lorne stares at her.

                    LORNE
          She's clean.

                    ANGEL
          You've been wrong before.

                    LORNE
          And I might be now. But she reads clean. Future's not
          too bright, but...

                    EVE
          What do you mean?

                    LORNE
          Hey, nothing's written in stone, lately, but if I was
          facing your future I'd make like Carmen Miranda and
          die.

They all start to leave.

                    EVE
          Wait. Please... are you gonna tell the Senior Partners
          where I am?

                    SPIKE
          Hell of a bargaining chip...

                    EVE
          They can't help you! I mean it, if...

                              ANGEL
          (seething)
          Give.

                              EVE
          You're talking about a sarcophagus that doesn't match
          anything in our records? There's nothing that's not in
          our records --
          (before they can speak)
          -- except what came before. The Old Ones.

                              ANGEL
          The original Demons. From before humankind. They were
          all driven out of this dimension.

                              EVE
          The ones that were still alive. But long before that,
          they were killing each other all the time and they
          don't die the way we do. Wesley may not know it, but
          his source books can conjure up anything, not just our
          own stock. Tell him to look for the texts that are
          forgotten, the oldest scrolls. You need to find the
          Deeper Well.

17 INT. WOLFRAM & HART - WESLEY'S OFFICE - DAY

The group is gathered once more. Gunn is bruised and cut, sitting heavily. Wes
at the desk, book before him. On the open page is text and a picture of the
sarcophagus.

                              WESLEY
          It's called Illyria. A great warrior king in the demon
          age. Murdered by rivals and left adrift in the Deeper
          Well.

                              ANGEL
          Which is what?

                              WESLEY
          A burial ground. The resting place of all the
          remaining Old Ones.

                              GUNN
          'Cept this one ain't resting.

                              WESLEY
          No. I don't think it's merely an infection. Fred's
          skin is... hardening. Like a shell. I think she's
          being hollowed out, so this thing can use her... to
          gestate. To claw its way back into the world. That's
          speculation. Either way she dies.

                              ANGEL
          Do we have any chance of finding this Deeper Well?

                              WESLEY
          I already have. It's in England, in the Cotswolds.
          (hands him a piece of paper)
          That's the location -- to the inch.

                              LORNE
          And here I made fun of all that book-learnin'.

                    WESLEY
          You just have to know to be looking for it.

                    ANGEL
          Lorne, tell Harmony to prep the jet.
          (to Spike)
          We can be there in ten hours.

                    KNOX
          You can be there in four.
          (off their looks)
          We have really good jets.

                    WESLEY
          It will have a guardian. Maybe several.

                    SPIKE
          Let 'em send an army.

                    GUNN
          How do we know going there is gonna do squat?

                    WESLEY
          The Deeper Well is almost like a prison for the dead.
          If something gets out, it's written that they can be
          drawn back. From the source.

                    ANGEL
          That's our shot.

                    WESLEY
          We'll keep working here, but, yes, I think it is.

                    LORNE
          (returning)
          If nobody thinks it's too ridiculous, I'm gonna go and
          pray.

                    WESLEY
          No, it's appreciated.
          (to Angel)
          Time is not on our side.

                    SPIKE
          Nobody's on our side.

                    ANGEL
          (to Spike)
          Come on. Let's save the day.

18 INT. WOLFRAM & HART - LOBBY

As the two of them exit, big-ass power shot.

19 INT. HOSPITAL ROOM - DAY

On Fred, in a delirium of pain. Her eyes open suddenly.

BLACK OUT

                    END OF ACT TWO

                    ACT THREE

20 INT. HOSPITAL ROOM - DAY

Wesley enters, book in hand, and goes to Fred's bed. It's empty.

21 INT. WOLFRAM & HART - LAB - DAY

A beaker shatters on the ground.

WIDEN to see Fred making her way to the computer, labcoat draped over her shoulders. She is so pale, and faint blue splotches are beginning to show on her skin.

She sits on a high stool and starts working the computer, having trouble focussing. She goes over to the table she left her glasses on, barely handing herself off from counter to counter, as Wesley enters at a good clip.

                    WESLEY
          Fred, you can't be doing this.

                    FRED
          (dismissive)
          Please, Wesley. I am exactly... the person to be doing
          this. Something could have been missed.

                    WESLEY
          Whatever it is that's happening we will stop it I
          swear to you.

79

                              FRED
                    I have to work.

                              WESLEY
                    You have to lie down!

                              FRED
                    I am not --
                    (Bitter tears spring into her eyes as she fires out)
                    I am not the damsel in distress, I'm not some case...
                    I have to work this thing. I lived in a cave for five
                    years, in a world where they killed my kind like
                    cattle. I'm not gonna be cut down by some monster flu.
                    I'm better than that.
                    (She looks at him defiantly a moment)
                    What a wonder.
                    (looks away)
                    How very scared I am.

He comes to her, leaves his book on the counter, saying:

                              WESLEY
                    I swear on my life that we will stop this. But you
                    must be back in bed. That's where I need you to
                    fight.

He tries to put his hands on her arms -- she jerks away --

                              FRED
                    Like I'm six years old --

-- and faints, Wes grabbing her, keeping her up. A moment and she focuses on him.

                              FRED (cont'd)
                    This is a house of death.
                    (looks at his book)
                    That can call up every book you need?

                              WESLEY
                    Every one.

                              FRED
                    Then bring it. Take me home.

22 INT. PRIVATE JET - DAY

Spike and Angel sit on either side, both looking out their respective windows.
Angel has his seatbelt on -- Spike is actually having trouble figuring his out.
They're both slightly nervous.

                              SPIKE
                    I've never flown before.

                              ANGEL
                    I've been in a helicopter... they don't... go this
                    high...

Beat.

                              SPIKE
                    Back to the mother country. After we save Fred we
                    should hit the West End, take in a show.

                              ANGEL
              I've never seen Les Miz...

                              SPIKE
              Trust me, halfway through the first act you'll be
              drinking humans again.

Beat.

                              ANGEL
              I can't lose her, Spike.

                              SPIKE
              You won't.

Angel looks out his window.

                              ANGEL
              I lost Cordy...

23 EXT. PRIVATE JET - CONTINUING

As it whips through the air.

24 INT. WOLFRAM & HART - GUNN'S OFFICE - DAY

Gunn is on the phone, agitated.

                              GUNN
              No, you're not hearing me. I know you got healers
              working for you... I don't care if the Old Ones scare
              them -- I don't care if the Old Ones **KILL** them, get
              their asses over here or you're gonna be in a world of
              hurt. No, I'm not talking lawsuit, I'm talking bones
              that go crunch. And if you --

The other party hangs up. Gunn looks at the phone, then slams it down.

                              KNOX
              We freeze her.

Gunn looks up as Knox enters:

                              KNOX (cont'd)
              Take her down to cryogenics... if we can't stop this,
              maybe we can just, you know, freeze it. In its tracks,
              until we come up with...

                              GUNN
              You know for sure you can do that?

                              KNOX
              Let's test it out.

25 INT. FRED'S BEDROOM - AFTERNOON

SERIES OF DISSOLVES

Wes carries Fred in and lays her on the bed. Wes wipes her face and arms with a
cloth. Wes reads his big mystical book as Fred sleeps. We are on that last as
he hears a slightly raspy voice:

                    FRED
        I finally get you up to my bedroom... and all you
        wanna do is read.

                    WESLEY
        You dozed off. Am I making too much noise?

                    FRED
        Not enough. I need noise to keep me here. Is it today?
        I mean...

                    WESLEY
        You only slept an hour.

                    FRED
        That's an hour I don't got now.

                    WESLEY
        Angel and Spike are on their way to finding your cure.
        I shouldn't like to be the thing standing in their way.

                    FRED
        And the bookman?

                    WESLEY
        The bookman came through. I think I gave them what
        they need. Now I'm just...
        (flips pages)
        looking...

                    FRED
        (sitting up)
        Feigenbaum!

                    WESLEY
        What?

                    FRED
        I have to find him! He's the master of... I have to
        have Feigenbaum here.

                    WESLEY
        Who is Feigenbaum?

Tears again in her eyes as she answers...

                    FRED
        I don't remember...

She breaks down and he holds her, trying to keep it together.

                    WESLEY
        Shhh... Sssshhhh......

A little while, and she comes back.

                    FRED
        Is it terrible, time like this, I'm worried how crappy
        I look?

                    WESLEY
        You're the most beautiful thing I've ever seen in my
        life.

                         FRED
            You always liked splotchy girls?

                         WESLEY
            It's my curse.

                         FRED
            Read to me.

                         WESLEY
            "The Dread Host's Compendium of Immortal Leeches?"

                         FRED
            Can that be any book in the world?

                         WESLEY
            Name one.

DISSOLVE TO:

26 INT. FRED'S BEDROOM - SUNSET

The room is redder, the shadows lengthening. Fred, lying, looks up at the
ceiling, while Wes reads softly:

                         WESLEY
            "She was such a little girl that one did not expect to
            see such a look on her small face. It would have been
            an old look for a child of twelve, and Sara Crewe was
            only seven. The fact was, however, that she was always
            dreaming and thinking odd things and could not herself
            remember any time when she had not been thinking
            things about grown up people and the world they
            belonged to. She felt as if she had lived a long, long
            time."

We end on the tableau: the woman in bed, the man beside her reading, the darken-
ing room.

27 EXT. ENGLISH COUNTRYSIDE - NIGHT

Trees and grass and the like. A car pulls up. Angel and Spike stepping out,
looking around them.

                         SPIKE
            When is a door not a door? When it's not sodding well
            there.

                         ANGEL
            That tree. Right there. You wanna bet that's the
            entrance to the Deeper Well?

                         SPIKE
            Either that or Christmasland...
            (off Angel's look)
            Don't you ever have any fun?

There is a flash, and two demon warriors are suddenly running at them from the
tree. They are dressed with a medieval bent, swords in hand, helmets covering
all but their grotesque mouths.

                         ANGEL
            I'm **about** to...

                         SPIKE
          And they even brought us weapons. Strategy?

                         ANGEL
          Just hold my hand. He holds out his hand.

Amused, Spike takes it in his. His eyes light up.

                         SPIKE
               (remembering)
          St. Petersburg.

                         ANGEL
          Thought you'd forgotten.

The warriors reach them and each man spins away and pulls taut the wire they
clasped -- the warriors charge headlong into it and are beheaded as cleanly as
Citoyen Capet.

They drop to the ground, heads rolling, as there is a flash and two more appear,
very similar in appearance. Angel and Spike both grab swords from the ground and
engage, making short work of them even as there is another flash, and another --
it's two to a man and still Angel and Spike are beyond efficient, brutal and
balletic.

28 INT. WOLFRAM & HART - LAB - NIGHT

Knox has a frozen bar held under the microscope, freezing smoke rising off it.
Gunn looks over his shoulder. A moment, then:

                         KNOX
          Dammit.

                         GUNN
          Don't say dammit. You got me all up in this Walt
          Disney mojo, don't tell me it's --

                         KNOX
          They're impervious. To cold. Her blood sample freezes
          but they just keep working like it's a sunny day in
          L.A. I'm sorry.

                         GUNN
          Okay, so it's a bust. What else we got?

                         KNOX
          I don't... it's hard to think, I'm so nervous. Look
          I'd never tell her this, but I care about Fred more
          than anyone I ever... she's like no one I've met, you
          know?

                         GUNN
          I do.

                         KNOX
          And nothing would make me happier than to be the white
          knight here. To have her look at me the way I... I
          don't just "care about" Fred. I practically worship it.

There is a beat. Gunn looks up.

                         GUNN
84   You said, "it."

                              KNOX
          What?

                         GUNN
          Not "her". You said, "I worship **it**."

A beat. Knox smiles.

                              KNOX
            Oops.

29 EXT. ENGLISH COUNTRYSIDE - NIGHT

The pile of bodies is considerably bigger now and Spike and Angel haven't let up for a second.

Angel guts the last one, turns and yells at the night:

                         ANGEL
Is that all? We haven't even started!

There is another flash -- and a LONE MAN in a sort of monk's robe appears. He is strong, middle-aged, a man out of time, with noble bearing and a beard with traces of grey.

                         DROGYN
            I'd say that's enough.

A beat, as the two look him over.

                         ANGEL
            Drogyn.

                         DROGYN
            Angel.

Spike looks at the two of them.

                         ANGEL
            You're the keeper of the Well.

                         DROGYN
          I have been for decades. It would not have been my
          first choice, but I go where they send me.

                         SPIKE
          Well who the hell are --

                         DROGYN
          Do not. Ask me a question. If you ever ask me a single
          question I will kill you outright and don't think for
          a moment that I can't.

                         ANGEL
          (to Spike)
          He can, he would.

                         SPIKE
          Heh?

                         DROGYN
          You're here about Illyria.

> ANGEL
>
> Yes.

> DROGYN
>
> You shouldn't have come.

> SPIKE
>
> (re: corpses)
> That's what they thought.

> DROGYN
>
> Yes. You're here, anyway. Walk in.

> SPIKE
>
> But how --

Drogyn turns sharply, murder in his eyes.

> DROGYN
>
> What did I just say to you not one minute ago? Don't. Ask.

He stalks off, causing an off-screen flash.

> ANGEL
>
> Seriously. He doesn't like questions.

> SPIKE
>
> Why the bloody hell not?

> ANGEL
>
> (leaving)
> He can't lie.

As Spike takes this in...

30 INT. WOLFRAM & HART - LAB - NIGHT

Knox crashes back into a bunch of equipment, Gunn holding his forearms. Knox isn't even putting up a fight. He is obscenely serene. Even cheerful. Gunn not so much.

> GUNN
>
> You did this! You did all of this!

> KNOX
>
> Technically, that's not the case. I just played my part --

> GUNN
>
> Why, you couldn't stand the thought of Wesley winning her so you kill her?

> KNOX
>
> (shakes free)
> No! I meant everything I said about her. I chose Fred because I love her. Because she's worthy. You think I'd have my God hatched out of some schmuck? This was all set in motion millions of years ago, Charles -- there's just no way to stop it.

                              GUNN
                 (sudden worry)
                 Angel and Spike --

                              KNOX
                 Oh, they're on the right track. That freaked me out,
                 Wes knocked it out of the park there -- but it doesn't
                 matter. Angel's not gonna save her.

                              GUNN
                 You don't know Angel.

                              KNOX
                 I'm not being clear. I don't mean Angel's gonna fail
                 to save her. I mean he's going to let her die.

Gunn stares at him.

BLACK OUT.

                         END OF ACT THREE

                         ACT FOUR

31 INT. CORRIDOR - NIGHT

Drogyn holds a torch -- the only light in the tiny, rounded stone corridor --
and moves at a brisk clip, the others following.

                              DROGYN
                 I never would have thought you'd end up here, Angel.

                              ANGEL
                 I could say the same.

                              SPIKE
                 So you two know each other.

Drogyn whips his head back.

                              SPIKE (cont'd)
                 (a little quickly --)
                 That's a statement. I already know that you do.

                              DROGYN
                 Angel and I have met.

                              ANGEL
                 Twice.
                 (to Drogyn)
                 We have no time here.

                              DROGYN
                 I'll tell you as much as I can. The Old Ones were
                 demons pure, and they warred as we would breathe,
                 endlessly. The greater ones were interned, for death
                 was not always their end. Some might rise again the
                 next day, some would lie in stasis for millennia.
                 Illyria was feared and beloved as few are. It was
                 lain to rest in the very depths of the Well. Until it
                 disappeared a month ago.

> SPIKE
> Someone took it from under your nose a month ago and
> you didn't miss it till now. That makes you quite the
> crap jailer, doesn't it?
> (defiantly, as Drogyn turns)
> Also a statement.

> DROGYN
> (to Angel)
> Your friend likes to talk.

> ANGEL
> So much he's even right sometimes. The man I remember
> couldn't be stolen from so easily.

> DROGYN
> The tomb was not stolen. It disappeared. I believe it
> was predestined to, as part of Illyria's escape plan.
> And as for my not noticing...

32 INT. THE DEEPER WELL CONTINUING

As they enter:

> DROGYN
> Well, my charges are not few.

As he says it, we see them stepping onto a bridge in a chamber lit from below
with an unearthly glow. Pull up and back to reveal that glow comes from an
endless tunnel down into the bowls of the earth. Six sarcophagi, all alien in
shape and design, float several feet below them. And six more below them. And
again, as far as the eye can make out.

Angel and Spike look down, amazed.

> SPIKE
> (whispers)
> Bloody Hell...

> ANGEL
> How far down does this go?

> DROGYN
> All the way. All the way through the earth.

The two of them take that in, then Angel turns to Drogyn
again.

> ANGEL
> So the coffin disappeared, teleported. But it was
> brought to us.

> DROGYN
> Illyria was a great power. So great that after
> millions of years dead, somewhere on this earth it
> still has acolytes.

33 INT. WOLFRAM & HART - LAB - NIGHT

Knox explains to Gunn:

                              KNOX
              There's just a few of us now. I came to L.A. because
              that's where I knew its kingdom had been. It was
              supposed to teleport to its base of power but the
              continents drifted, which they do. I had others help
              me get it here and it was stuck in -- would you
              believe it -- customs. But you took care of that.

Gunn's anger drains into a quiet horror. And Knox pulls a piece of paper from
his pocket to confirm Gunn's worst fear.

                              KNOX (cont'd)
              You signed the order that brought it to this lab so
              you could get another brain-boost. Like I said, I was
              only one small part. Of a great machine.

Gunn starts pacing around, unable to accept what he's hearing

                              GUNN
              Angel's gonna save her.

                              KNOX
              What he's fighting against is older than the concept
              of time. I couldn't stop it. There's nothing to do now
              but wait. Wait and try to figure out exactly what you
              want to tell your friends about what happened --

Gunn SLAMS the microscope into Knox's head, knocking him clean out. Drops down
and continues hitting him, murder in his eyes.

34 INT. FRED'S BEDROOM - NIGHT

Fred screams in pain, her body rippling with crusting agony.

Wes pulls out a syringe from a packet marked MORPHINE, tries to grab her arm.
Her veins are easy to find -- but the needle breaks on it.

                              FRED
              AhHAAHoh God I've sinned, I've sinned and I'm being
              punished, I don't know what's wrong I never got a
              B- before, I'm sorry I'm sorry make it stop...

Her babble ends in dry retching. Wesley looks at her, helpless, but the pain
subsides. She looks around, seeing him.

                              FRED (cont'd)
              Why did we go there? Why did we think we could beat
              it? It's evil, Wesley. It's bigger than anything.

                              WESLEY
              (tears welling)
              I don't believe that.

She scrambles back against the wall, crouched.

                              FRED
              (to the air)
              I 'm with him!
              (to Wesley)

You won't leave me now. We're so close.

                    WESLEY
I will never leave you.

                    FRED
OOh, that was bad. But it's better now. You won't
leave me.

                    WESLEY
I won't.

                    FRED
My boys... I walk with heroes, think about that.

                    WESLEY
You are one.

                    FRED
Superhero. This is my power. To **not let them take me.**
Not me.

                    WESLEY
That's right.

                    FRED
(quietly)
That's right.

A long moment, as she relaxes a bit. She shakily takes Wes's hand, holds it to
her breast.

                    FRED (cont'd)
He's with me.

90

35 INT. THE DEEPER WELL - NIGHT

Drogyn looks disturbed.

                    DROGYN
          It's been freed. The demon's essence.

                    SPIKE
          Yes, it's been freed -- Why do you think we're here?

Drogyn glares.

                    SPIKE (cont'd)
          And what's your favorite color? What's your favorite
          song? Who's the goalkeeper for Manchester United and
          (two-finger salute)
          How many fingers am I holding up? You wanna kill me,
          try. I don't have time for your quirks. This thing, this
          dead thing is in our friend. Now how do we get it out?

                    ANGEL
          Answer.

                    DROGYN
          (indicating the next chamber)
          The power to draw Illyria back lies in there. It
          requires a champion who has traveled from where it
          lies to where it belongs.

                    ANGEL
          You got two of those right here.

                    DROGYN
          But I didn't know it was free. It's in your friend.

                    SPIKE
          Cookin' her organs, yeah, let's move.

                    DROGYN
          We can save her --

                    SPIKE
          Then get on the --

                    DROGYN
          But there's a price.

                    ANGEL
          There's no price I won't pay.

                    DROGYN
          You **won't** pay, because you're already dead. It can't
          use you.

                    ANGEL
          Tell us.

                    DROGYN
          If we draw the sarcophagus back to the Well Illyria
          will be drawn out of your friend. And into every
          single person between here and there. Whether or not
          the beast succeeds in hatching inside your friend, it
          is stuck there. But we draw it out -- it would be the

mystical equivalent of "airborne". It will claw into
every soul in its path to keep from being trapped
entire. Tens, maybe hundreds of thousands will become
lesser hosts. Will die in agony. If you save her. This
sits.

> ANGEL
> No.

> DROGYN
> I'm sorry.

> SPIKE
> That's madness.

> DROGYN
> This is the place of madness. It's your friend's life,
> or... so many others.

Beat.

> I'll prepare the spell. It's your call.

He exits. The men say nothing. A moment, and Spike slams
his fist down on the railing, time after time.

Another silence.

> ANGEL
> The Hell with the world.

He stalks off after Drogyn.

36 INT. FRED'S BEDROOM - NIGHT

Fred is huddled on the bed, shaking slightly. When she
speaks, she's weaker than before, but more coherent.

> FRED
> Will you read to me some more?

> WESLEY
> Of course, I --

> FRED
> The light hurts my eyes. But I don't want you to
> turn it off. But it hurts my eyes. Everything's so
> bright and hollow... I thought it was supposed to get
> dimmer... Cavemen win. Of **course** the cavemen win.

She gasps, arching back, and breathes shakily for a moment. He moves closer to
support her... her voice betrays her pain...

> FRED (cont'd)
> I can't do this, this isn't right... there's so many
> things I had to say. I have opinions on several
> issues... I never... except for the five years I spent
> in a hell dimension I've never been outside the U.S.
> I've never worked the word "dodecahedron" into a
> sentence without it sounding really forced.
> (suddenly urgent)
> I'm never gonna love you. I could've loved you, I
> would have, I have to say that to you --

WESLEY
I'm gonna remind you of that in
the morning...

FRED
Yes, Angel's gonna save me and
make me feel a fool...

37 INT. THE DEEPER WELL - NIGHT

Angel stands in the doorway, his back to
us. He has not made it through.

A moment and he turns back, moves toward
Spike, helpless admission in his eyes.

ANGEL
Spike...

SPIKE
(he already knows)
This goes all the way through to
the other side. So I figure
there's a bloke somewhere around
New Zealand, standing on a bridge
like this one and looking back
down at us. All the way down.
(softly)
There's a hole in the world. Feel
like we ought to have known.

Angel says nothing. He can't.

38 INT. FRED'S BEDROOM - NIGHT

FRED
Will you kiss me?

Wesley does, softly. They stay close.

FRED (cont'd)
Would you have loved me?

WESLEY
(smiles softly)
I've loved you since I've known
you. No, it's not... I think maybe
even before.

FRED
I'm so sorry --

WESLEY
No, no...

She arches again, coughing.

> FRED
> You have to talk to my parents. They need to know that
> I wasn't scared... that it was quick, that I wasn't
> scared -- **kkkkkah** --oh god --

> WESLEY
> You have to fight. You don't have to talk, just
> concentrate on fighting, just hold on...

> FRED
> I'm not scared I'm not scared I'm not scared --
> Wesley... please, why can't I stay...

He buries his face in her neck, succumbing. She stares out into nothing, sees
nothing. Ceases.

> WESLEY
> Please... please...

A moment more, holding her, and he realizes that she is dead. He remains
motionless, wrapped in her.

There is a pause.

EXTREME CLOSE ON: HER EYE. Open, dead. A blue frost suddenly, cracklingly covers
the whole eyeball.

She bucks like a greenbroke horse, throws him off in the power of it, thrashing
and twitching on the ground for a few moments -- he reaches for her --

ANGLE: She rises into an empty frame, all the fear gone from her face. Her new
face.

Her eyes are blue, patterned without pupils. A similar color has creeped in at
the edges of her face in a striking mottle that has even bled streaks of blue
into her hair.

Wesley, still on the ground, looks up at her, hope giving way to horror.

She looks at her hands. At her new body. She speaks without undo emphasis.

> ILLYRIA
> This will do.

BLACK OUT.

<u>THE END</u>

ANGEL
"A Hole in the World"

<u>SET LIST INTERIORS</u>

BURKLE HOUSEHOLD
        FRED'S ROOM

BASEMENT

WOLFRAM & HART
        LAB
        GUNN'S OFFICE
        ANGEL'S OFFICE
        UPSTAIRS/LOBBY
        LOBBY
        WESLEY'S OFFICE
        WHITE ROOM

HOSPITAL ROOM

LINDSEY'S BEDROOM

PRIVATE JET

FRED'S BEDROOM

CORRIDOR

THE DEEPER WELL

<u>EXTERIORS</u>

BURKLE HOME - DAY

WOLFRAM & HART - DAY

PRIVATE JET - DAY

ENGLISH COUNTRYSIDE - NIGHT

ANGEL

issue three

scriptbook ™

Episode
SPIN THE BOTTLE

Written By
JOSS WHEDON

ANGEL™
"SPIN THE BOTTLE"

WRITTEN BY

JOSS WHEDON

Starring:
DAVID BOREANAZ
CHARISMA CARPENTER
ALEXIS DENISOF
J. AUGUST RICHARDS
AMY ACKER
VINCENT KARTHEISER
ANDY HALLETT
KAM HESKIN
SVEN HOLMBERG

Created By
JOSS WHEDON
&
DAVID GREENWALT

Written and Directed By
JOSS WHEDON

TEASER

1 INT. CLUB - NIGHT

Lorne is on stage, crooning. It's small and minimalist: stool, mic, drink. We hear (but do not see) light club crowd noises.

                         LORNE
              (sings)
              MEMORIES, LIKE THE CORNER OF MY MIND... etc. ...OF
              THE WAY WE WERE...
              (speaks)
              Ah, youth. Is there anything more magical? A time of
              first loves, of great discoveries, of taut, firm,
              supple yet perky - well let's face it; youth is it.
              It's a national obsession, Krazy kats - everyone's
              trying to touch it, reclaim it or freeze dry it so it
              never goes away. But somewhere between the boob-jobs,
              the chin-tucks and the horn sharpenings - not me,
              sweeties, that was Mr. Spelling - somewhere people all
              forget what a mess youth is. It' s a time of magic,
              all right, and there is nothing more unreliable or
              annoying than magic. Let me tell you a little story.
              Starts with a kid —

2 EXT. STREET - NIGHT

Connor walks along, miserable. Loud, painwracked rock blares as he skulks down the street. Images —(already shot)— of Cordy, of them sleeping, of them kissing, flash Angel-style in his brain. He bumps into a bigger guy, doesn't give, doesn't break stride. Mounting fury.

We Freeze on him:

                         LORNE (V.O.)
              Actually, no. It really starts here:

3 INT. ANGEL'S HOTEL - COURTYARD - NIGHT
(Continues from the end of Episode 5)

                         CORDELIA
              Were we in love?

                         ANGEL
              Urn...

                         CORDELIA
              Were we?

                         ANGEL
              What?

                         CORDELIA
              In love!

                         ANGEL
              With each other?

                         CORDELIA
              Mister, if you start giving me the runaround-

                    ANGEL
          I'm not! I'm not.

                    CORDELIA
          Then tell me the truth.

                    ANGEL
          I don't know.

                    CORDELIA
          You don't know?

                    ANGEL
          Well, I'm not sure.

                    CORDELIA
          Now I kinda think that's the sort of thing I'd
          remember. Hey, maybe you wrote it down somewhere! A
          note on the fridge, maybe...

                    ANGEL
          I do remember, I just... I had feelings for you. And I
          thought that maybe you... but you never told me. You
          asked me to meet you, to talk, and I never saw you
          again.

                    CORDELIA
          And you think I wanted to meet you to tell you that I
          was in love with you?

                    ANGEL
          Cordy, I really don't think you're ready to be dealing
          with this.

                    CORDELIA
          Or maybe I was gonna tell you to "back off, buddy."
          Maybe you were coming on too strong - harassing me in
          the workplace! Maybe I had a red hot restraining order
          in my mitts, you ever think of that?

                    ANGEL
          I was never... in the workplace, I- well, there was
          that one time with the ballet and the stripping and
          the roundness - but that was a spell, and we were
          meeting on the bluffs in Malibu at night! That's a
          pretty romantic restraining order.

                    CORDELIA
          Don't yell at me! You're yelling at me.

                    ANGEL
          I'm not - see, this is why I don't wanna answer
          questions I don't have the answer for. All I know
          is that you were my dearest friend. And I just hope
          that... I want that back. That much at least.

The mood has quieted.

                    CORDELIA
          You have no idea how much this is killing me. I know
          my ABC's, my history... I know who's president and
          that I sort of wish I didn't... I know the name of

every shoe store in the Beverly Center but I don't...
(welling up)
I don't even recognize the sound of my own name.

He sits by her.

                    ANGEL
          We'll get you back. No matter what, I promise you we
          will.

                    LORNE
          (entering)
          Who is "we", paleface? I'm the one out there doing the
          legwork.

They turn as he joins them, chipper as a cheerleader.

                    LORNE (cont'd)
          Well, it was really more "lapwork", 'cause guess what
          just fell into it?

                    CORDELIA
          What?

                    LORNE
          (producing a small earthenware bottle)
          A memory spell, provided by one of my clients - that
          is guaranteed to get our Cordy back to the way she
          was.

                    ANGEL
          Guaranteed?

                    LORNE
          No pain, no side effects - I'm telling you, swingers -
          there's no way this can fail.

4 INT. CLUB - NIGHT

Lorne just stares at the camera a beat.

                    LORNE
          So I'm an idiot. What are you, perfect?

                    END OF TEASER

                    ACT ONE

5 INT. CLUB - NIGHT

Lorne takes a sip, continues.

                    LORNE
          The fact is, I had every reason to believe this spell
          would work. And it did! After a fashion. What happened
          during it, and what came after...

We cut in close as he takes a moment.

                    LORNE (cont'd)
          Ooh, I'm gonna need a bigger drink.
          (back into the story)

>   But the spell was legit, straight up. I had it off
>   this Wraith - sweet girl, not overly tangible but she
>   deals in memory spells professionally.

The camera has come around, the lighting's changed and we see we're in:

6 INT. ANGEL'S HOTEL - COURTYARD - CONTINUING

>   LORNE
>   She swears up and down that with the right mix we can
>   stop this talking and cut to the Cordelia Chase in two
>   ticks of a ticking thing!

>   ANGEL
>   I don't know. Spells... I don't trust 'em.

>   CORDELIA
>   And I don't care. I'm in.

>   ANGEL
>   Cordy, you can't just-

>   CORDELIA
>   I don't care. Pain, side effects - this thing turns me
>   into Mousaka I'm happy - as long as I can remember
>   that I'm a Mousaka.

>   LORNE
>   Don't even worry about it, princess. I've got all the
>   ingredients ready. As soon as we gather the six, we're
>   good to go.

>   ANGEL
>   The six what?

7 INT. WESLEY'S APARTMENT - NIGHT

On a card that reads: "As per your specs. Happy Hunting - Emil." Widen to
see Wesley holding the card, a sleazy young delivery guy waiting, and a box
containing various items: a pair of what look like compact night-vision
goggles, some other weapons (TBD). The room is still a bit trashed from
the portal in Ep. 5.

Wesley already has a device strapped to his arm. It's a - deringer-stake-thing,
but unlike any we've seen on the show - impossibly compact, sleek, metal -
making it work may require some CGI. Wes whips out his arm and it does, shooting
out from the wrist (from the back of the hand). Wes makes a fist and it fires
and splinters a vase sticking into the wall.

>   WESLEY
>   Gift from my aunt. Always hated that thing.

He flicks his wrist back and from the front of his hand a sword telescopes and
unfolds (Definite CGI). He gives it a swing, then retracts it. Pulls out a bun-
dle of money and tosses it to the young man.

>   WESLEY (cont'd)
>   Tell Emil if it tests all right in the field, he'll be
>   hearing from me again.

> DELIVERY GUY
> Yeah,- okay. He'll be thrilled.

The kid leaves, Wesley picking up the goggles as the phone rings. He picks it up.

> WESLEY
> Price here.

He throws the goggles onto his couch as he listens.

> WESLEY (cont'd)
> Yes.
> (beat)
> Lorne, I said yes. I'll be there right away. If it works, it's worth doing. All right. Is everything else... is everyone there?
> (listens)
> No, I just wanted to know if everything was... all right with Fred.

8 INT. ANGEL'S HOTEL - FRED AND GUNN'S ROOM - NIGHT

Well, no. She and Gunn lie side by side in bed, both looking straight up, him shirtless, her in a sleepin' tee. Acres of distance between them.

After a big while:

> FRED
> I'm gonna make some cocoa.

She gets up, heads for the door.

> GUNN
> I'll take some too.

She turns to look at him, a little surprised.

> GUNN (cont'd)
> If you don't mind...

> FRED
> No, you just never have cocoa.

> GUNN
> Lotta firsts tonight.

> FRED
> Charles, I-

> GUNN
> Let's don't. Not now.

A beat,

and then she opens the door. Angel is standing right in front of her.

A beat.

> FRED
> See ordinarily, that's the sort of thing would make me scream.

> ANGEL
> I didn't know if this was a bad time...

> GUNN
> (still looking at the ceiling)
> And what better way to find out than sneaking up and listenin' in?

> FRED
> (to Angel)
> What do you want?

9 INT. ANGEL'S HOTEL - LOBBY - NIGHT

FROM ABOVE - a mystical circle has been drawn, Lome crossing through it, putting on finishing touches.

TILT UP to see Gunn and Fred entering, dressed.

> GUNN
> Oh, good, symbols on the floor. That always goes well.

> LORNE
> Check your sarcasm at the door, pouty - britches. This is for Cordy.

> GUNN
> I just don't want no portals opening around here. Had enough of that crap.

Lorne shoots him a look as Gunn crosses into the office.

> FRED
> Sorry, Lorne. We really have had a whole lot of that crap.

> LORNE
> Oh, my parade is rain-proofed, baby doll. First reading since my head got drilled and I find the spell that's gonna bring our little Cordy right back to us.
> (in Pylean)
> Lo-lath ch-owmg ne bruun.

> FRED
> (smiling)
> Kaya-No-m'tek.

> WESLEY
> Did I miss the spell? Did English go away?

He is standing in the doorway. Fred and Lorne turn to him as he approaches, Lorne blithely, Fred less so.

> LORNE
> It's Pylean, crumpet. I said "I may be prepared to shout a joyful chant."

Fred is locked in to Wes, not paying attention to the smalltalk she's making. In the b.g., Gunn appears in the office doorway, remaining unseen. (The more obsessive of us may realize they are in nearly the same configuration as they were right before they went to the Ballet.)

                    FRED
          And I said "May your words please the Gods."

                    WESLEY
          Are you all right? Did you-

                    FRED
          It's done.

10 INT. CLUB - NIGHT

                    LORNE
          Okay, first of all she didn't say "May your words
          please the Gods" so much as "May you orally please the
          Gods", which is a slight... inflection is very crucial
          in our - but God bless her, it's always nice to hear
          the Mother tongue. As long as it's not from my mother.
          (beat re: mic)
          Is this on?
          (business)
          Secondly. I didn't know that a couple of hours ago
          Fred had tried to kill her evil professor by opening
          a portal.

11 INT. ANGEL'S HOTEL - LOBBY - NIGHT

Everyone is holding still (not frozen) as the camera rushes them as they're described. (NOTE: This will be shot two ways: Once with Lome holding still, his monologue working as V.O., and once with him actually explaining in the room.)

                    LORNE
          Gunn didn't know that Wesley had helped her. Wesley
          didn't know that Gunn had killed the guy himself to
          save Fred from becoming a killer. And Fred didn't know
          that Gunn was right then figuring out that Wesley had
          helped her try.

12 INT. CLUB - NIGHT

                    LORNE
          So you can see I didn't have all the facts when I
          started this. It's my job to read people, but nobody
          in this clan was exactly singing. And me, hey I was
          thinking about Cordelia.

13 INT. ANGEL'S HOTEL - CORDY'S ROOM - NIGHT

Cordy enters from the bathroom in a towel, is startled to see Angel there.

                    CORDELIA
          Oh!

                    ANGEL
          Hey. Oh. Sorry.

                    CORDELIA
          Wanted to clean up. Connor and I not exactly staying
          at the Mondrian.

107

                    ANGEL
          How is he?

                    CORDELIA
          He's seventeen. He's a mess.
          (takes a beat)
          There's a lot of pain in him. I think it helps, having
          me there.

                    ANGEL
          (not thrilled)
          Good. That's good. We're almost ready.

                    CORDELIA
          Do I have to wear some froufy ceremonial gown or
          something?

                    ANGEL
          No, no. Come as you are. I mean, not as you are, but
          with clothes. Of your choosing. I'll be downstairs.

He starts to go.

                    CORDELIA
          So you're perfectly okay with just wandering into
          my room any old time. That fits the "we were in
          love" theory and the "harassment" theory pretty much
          equally.

                    ANGEL
          Hopefully, that'll all be answered soon.

He exits. She unwraps the towel and we cut to:

14 INT. ANGEL'S HOTEL - OFFICE NIGHT

Fred and Wes are helping Lorne with last-minute fixes. Fred points to something
they need in the office. Wes heads in and grabs it, doesn't see Gunn sitting in
the shadows at first.

                    GUNN
          So I guess I'm the muscle, huh?

Wesley turns, not overplaying insouciance.

                    WESLEY
          Sorry?

                    GUNN
          Angel's the man on the card, it's his world, I ain't a
          leader no more. Don't got that Champion's heart, like
          Cordy - and the brains, well, that was you. So that
          leaves muscle.

                    WESLEY
          What about Fred?

                    GUNN
          Well, that's the question, isn't it? She's pretty
          brainy, too. Maybe you two are kindred souls. Maybe
          that's why she went to you for help gettin' revenge
          on that Professor. Killin' takes brains.

                    WESLEY
        I did what you weren't prepared to do.

Gunn rising, slow burn:

                    GUNN
        You have no idea what I've - what I would do for her.

                    WESLEY
        Is there some reason I should need to know?

                    GUNN
        You think I don't smell this a mile off? You think I
        don't know why you keep running back here?

                    WESLEY
        Because you keep needing my help.

                    GUNN
        I'm gonna say this once: You move on Fred, I'm a put
        you down hard.

                    WESLEY
        I'm glad to see you have such faith in your
        relationship.

                    GUNN
        Keep pushing, English.

Wes raises a dismissive arm.

                    WESLEY
        Do you think you could get out of my way?

                    GUNN
        (overlapping)
        What's to stop me from pushing your face in right —

He grabs Wes' arm as he says it - and the slim, nasty tech-stake snaps out,
inches from Gunn's face. Beat.

                    WESLEY
        Not all of us have muscle to fall back on.

He snaps the stake back. Gunn lets go, and Wes starts to pass him.

                    GUNN
        What happened to you, man?

Wes looks at him, says simply:

                    WESLEY
        I had my throat cut and all my friends abandoned me.

And he walks out.

15 INT. ANGEL'S HOTEL - LOBBY - NIGHT

The group sits in a circle, camera on each of their less-than-happy faces as
Lorne walks behind them, sprinkling them with tiny amounts of powder.

                        LORNE
            Now we represent the six spheres of consciousness,
            the six gifts from the Lords of Shah-teyaman, the
            six walls of the house of truth. We're all one with
            Cordelia, we bring to this circle only trust and
            imagination.

He sits, continuing.

                    LORNE (cont'd)
            The bottle in the center of the
            circle contains the liquid essence
            that has passed through the wraith
            and been gathered here —

                    GUNN
            We're curing Cordy with a urine
            sample?

                  CORDELIA
            Okay, not drinking it...

                    LORNE
Hush, puppies. All we do is join hands and
concentrate. On the bottle, on Cordy, on calling
her back to the way she was.

                    ANGEL
            Let's do it.

Tentatively, they all join hands.

                    LORNE
            Eyes on the bottle.
            (quietly)
            We come in supplication and hope.
            Bring her back.

They sit. They stare.

ANGLE: The bottle begins to shake. A wisp of smoke starts to drift from the top.

Cordy stares at it, apprehensive, almost pleading... The bottle shakes more.
Everybody stares. Cordy's hand squeezes Angel's.

The bottle starts spinning like a top, more smoke coming out and then — whoosh!
It topples to its side and spins around, spewing smoke at all of them. The smoke
CGI absorbs into all of them simultaneously, knocking them back and breaking the
circle.

Then shit goes trippy. We start getting some serious tracers on these folks,
their voices distorted, all of them disoriented and in various stages of weird,
(not CGI).

                  CORDELIA
            What's going on...?

                    LORNE
            Feel a little...

Lorne wanders off behind the counter — and passes out.

110 Fred looks at Wes and Gunn, whom she is between, and moves over into the corner.

                    GUNN
          What's happening to us?

                    CORDELIA
            Is this poison?

Angel wanders off as well, into the

16 EXT. ANGEL'S HOTEL - GARDEN - CONTINUING

Where he looks up at the stars, breathing deep.

                    ANGEL
            Found me, did you...

17 EXT. ANGEL'S HOTEL - LOBBY - CONTINUING

Fred is hanging onto the wall near a potted plant.

                    FRED
          This is important, it's so beautiful...

Then she barfs.

                    WESLEY
          (laughs quietly to himself)
          We'll just wait to see if there's any side-effects...

Cordy is freaking out —

                    CORDELIA
          What's happening? We can't just... we have to... NO!

And she steps hard on the clay bottle, crushing it.

A CGI WHOOSH moment, then everybody stops. The four of them still in the room
take a moment, then look at each other.

Wes looks at Cordy.

                    CORDELIA (cont'd)
          Okay, what the hell is going on here?

                    WESLEY
          What's your name?

                    CORDELIA
          I'm Cordelia Chase, dumb-ass, and if this is some sort
          of sophomore hazing prank where I get doped up and
          left with a bunch of proto-losers, then my parents are
          gonna be suing the entire population of Sunnydale,
          comprende?

                    GUNN
          What the Hell are you talking about?

                    CORDELIA
          It's called kidnapping a minor, hair - club for men,
          and if you think for a second I'm putting up with it,
          you don't know... Cordelia...

Angel has come in from the garden, a bit dazed.

CORDELIA (cont'd)
(to herself)
Hello, Salty Goodness.

END OF ACT ONE

ACT TWO

18 INT. ANGEL'S HOTEL - LOBBY - NIGHT

Where we left off.

                    WESLEY
All right. Hold on. You're Cordelia Chase. You're a
high school student, you live in Sunnydale.

                    CORDELIA
Right.

                    WESLEY
(to Gunn)
So who are you?

                    GUNN
I'm the guy gonna be kicking a whole mess a' ass,
somebody don't tell me what's going on.

                    CORDELIA
(oh come on)
Well, what do they call you for short?

                    WESLEY
Does anyone here recognize anyone?

                    FRED
Uh, I'm Fred Burkle...
(to Cordy, smiling tentatively)
I'm also a sophomore, at Woodrow Wilson in San
Anton'...

                    CORDELIA
We're both sophomores? Gosh, let's be best friends so
I can lose all my cool ones!

                    WESLEY
There's no call to be snippety, miss.

                    CORDELIA
This is the clarion call for snippety. Princess
Charles.

                    WESLEY
It's Wesley, thank you. Wyndam - Price. I'm from the
Watcher's Academy in Southern Hampshire. In fact, I
happen to be Head Boy.

                    CORDELIA
Gee, I wonder how you earned THAT nickname.

                    WESLEY
          (totally doesn't get it)
          A lot of effort, I don't mind saying.

                    GUNN
          Gunn.

                    WESLEY
          Where? Oooh! Gun?

                    GUNN
          Me. That's my name.
          (to Cordy)
          The short version.

                    WESLEY
          And what school do you attend?

Gunn stares at him for a beat.

                    CORDELIA
          (to Angel)
          So we've heard from the socially handi-capable, what's
          your story?

Angel has just been staring, his brain reeling. He utters softly:

                    ANGEL
          Mad. You're all mad.

                    FRED
          We're a little testy, but we do seem to have been
          kidnapped.

                    ANGEL
          These clothes, your speech, this place... what land is
          this?

                    GUNN
          What land is it supposed to be?

                    WESLEY
          Yes, where do you hail from, friend?

                    ANGEL
          I'm not your friend, English pig. We never wanted
          you in Ireland and we don't want you now.

                    GUNN
          You're Irish?

                    CORDELIA
          You don't sound Irish.

                    ANGEL
          For most certain I sound exactly like...(realizes he
          doesn't). There's something wrong with my voice.

                    WESLEY
          Well, what's your name?

                    ANGEL
          Liam.

                    CORDELIA
          Great, we've all got names! Bye now.

                    WESLEY
          I wouldn't be so quick. Miss Chase, to leave. Clearly
          we're all the victims of some nefarious scheme.

Angel touches his throat, listening to himself speak.

                    ANGEL
          Liam. Liiiammm. Gaaalllllway. "Hail Mary, full of
          grace...."

                    WESLEY
          I'll lay odds that door is bolted shut. And who knows
          what peril lies outside it? Before we do anything, I
          suggest we gather as much information as we can.

                    CORDELIA
          And I suggest we gather some cops!

                    GUNN
          I don't want any heat near me.

                    FRED
          I don't know if we should go to the police, anyhow. I
          mean, they're probably involved.

                    GUNN
          In what?

                    FRED
          Well, don't y'all think this is some kind of
          government conspiracy? 'Cause my friend Levon says
          the government's always taking kids and experimenting
          on them.
          (remembers)
          Did anybody else have to take a personality disorder
          test recently? They ask you about politics, and your
          bowel movements, and if you wanna be a florist —

                    CORDELIA
          Okay! We've heard from Scarlett O'Please-shut-me-up.
          Does anyone sane have a theory?

                    FRED
          (grumbling)
          There's conspiracies and stuff. You don't even know.

                    GUNN
          I got no problem with the idea that the Man is messing
          with us.

                    WESLEY
          The important thing is to start with the facts. We're
          all from different cities, we're all of an age...
          (feels his face)
          Judging from the amount of facial hair I've grown, we
          must have been unconscious for at least a month.

Cordy, following his lead, touches herself — and freaks.

CORDELIA
Oh, God, oh god... my hair! My hair!
(starting to cry)
The government gave me bad hair!

FRED
No, no, it's nice!

WESLEY
Yes, it's just the thing.

CORDELIA
Are you sure?

WESLEY
It's very attractive. But a clue, nonetheless. Perhaps
the whole point of this experiment is hair.

GUNN
I vote he's not in charge.

ANGEL
(quietly)
It's the devil.

They'd pretty much forgotten him. He sits on the steps, lost and alone. He looks
at them.

ANGEL (cont'd)
It's the Devil.

CORDELIA
My hair?

ANGEL
My father said I was a sinner, that I'd come to a bad
end... and now I've come to Hell.

GUNN
(looking around)
Well, Hell's a lot nicer 'n my place.

WESLEY
It appears to be some sort of hotel.

FRED
Well then maybe it's Motel Hell!

She snorts with laughter. Not joined by others.

FRED (cont'd)
There's a movie...

WESLEY
Well, let's get the lay of the place.

GUNN
Man, don't be giving me orders. I run my own crew.

WESLEY
I'm sure your seafaring adventures are very
interesting, but I have experience in things you
couldn't imagine. I'm not Head Boy for nothing.

GUNN
You're gonna be Headless Boy, you stay in my face.

                    WESLEY
                (nervous)
                Intimidation? Points for effort.
                (karate pose)
                Perhaps a little KaraTAY technique will put you in
                your place.

He waves his arms like an idiot. Strikes a pose and his stake pops out right in
front of his own face.

                    WESLEY (cont'd)
                MMNAHH! Oh. Ah. Ooh.

                    CORDELIA
                What the Hell's that?

                    WESLEY
                A clue.

                    GUNN
                That a wooden stake you got?

Wes pushes it back in.

                    WESLEY
                Apparently, yes. Which changes the scenario quite a
                bit.

Fred apes Wesley's moves — but nothing pops out.

                    FRED
                I didn't get one.

                    GUNN
                Nobody got one 'cept English here. Why's that?

                    WESLEY
                I don't know, but I suggest we all look about for
                weapons of some kind.

                    GUNN
                That part works.

He casts about, as does Fred, who goes behind the counter.

We hold Wes in the foreground, testing his stake, flexing to pop it out again —
and Fred trips over something with a shriek — drops out of frame as Wes jerks
at the noise, his sword popping out and unfolding — he shrieks as it folds back
in and Fred pops back up into frame, again with the shrieking and turning and
running and right into Gunn.

                    WESLEY
                All right!

He turns slowly, holding his arms out, away from his body.

                    WESLEY (cont'd)
                Nobody scream. Or touch my arms.

> FRED
> Well, I think I found another clue.

Cordy joins them. Wesley slowly pulls up his pants legs, makes sure they're safe.

> GUNN
> She's not wrong.

> CORDELIA
> Okay, this is even less funny.

Wesley joins them.

> CORDELIA (cont'd)
> What the Hell is that?

They are all looking at:

The prone body of the still-unconscious Lorne. Angel is the last to join them, looks at it tentatively.

> ANGEL
> I knew it. It's the Devil.

> FRED
> How come the devil's sleeping?

19 EXT. ALLEY - NIGHT

A vampire goes flying into frame, crashing into garbage cans. Another backs off, threatened but still tough. Behind him, their intended victim, a hooker named LOLA, cowers.

> VAMPIRE
> This ain't your business, kid.

REVERSE ON: Connor. Dead pissed.

> CONNOR
> No...

He whip kicks the guy, gut punches him seven times in a second.

> CONNOR (cont'd)
> This is just my bad mood.

He tosses the one into the approaching other. As they rise he jumps between them, split kick to both their heads, lands, whips out a stake —

> CONNOR (cont'd)
> This is my business.

— and dusts one. The other runs away. Connor moves to the girl.

> CONNOR (cont'd)
> Are you hurt?

> LOLA
> They were gonna kill me... bastards...

                    CONNOR
          You're safe now.

He says it deadpan, leaving. She puts a hand to his arm.

                    LOLA
          Whoah, whoah! Hey, baby, you saved my life! So young,
          and so strong... (cozies up to him) Don't you want
          your reward?

Actually, he does. But he's not sure how to handle this. Looks at her as she
pushes herself against him.

                    LOLA (cont'd)
          I could give you a nice reward...

                    CONNOR
          I... yeah. Okay.

                    LOLA
          You got fifty bucks?

                    CONNOR
          What for?

She pushes off him.

                    LOLA
          You got nothin'.

                    CONNOR
          I saved you.

                    LOLA
          You still don't ride free, junior. Why don't you run
          home to mama, maybe she'll give you a special treat
          for being such a good boy.

She leaves. He burns.

20 INT. CLUB - NIGHT

                    LORNE
          Classy girl. And poor Connor: engine revving and stuck
          in park. Well, enough about him. In the meanwhile,
          guess what I'm doing for fun?

21 INT. ANGEL'S HOTEL - LOBBY - NIGHT

Lorne is still unconscious. Wesley is putting the finishing touches on majorly
tying him to a chair.

                    GUNN
          I say we cut off his head.

                    WESLEY
          He might have information we need. When' he wakes up —

                    GUNN
          When he wakes up we don't even know if those ropes are
          gonna hold him. I say cut off his damn head.

                    WESLEY
        Thank you, Marie Antoinette, but since you're —

                         GUNN
            What'd you call me?

                         CORDELIA
            Hey! Hey! You two wanna pause the homo-erotic buddy
            cop session long enough to explain this? Wooden
            stakes, a guy with horns — and neither of you seems
            that surprised when things just keep getting weirder.

She indicates:

ANGLE: THROUGH THE WEAPONS CABINET
Fred and Angel stare at it.

                              FRED
                    They really are.
                    (to Angel)
                    Have you got any weed?

He has no idea what she's talking about. Wes addresses the group:

                         WESLEY
            All right. I'm going to let you in on something you
            may have trouble comprehending. But I assure you that
            however -

                         GUNN
            Vampires are real.

                         WESLEY
            I was telling!

                         GUNN
            There's vampires all over L.A. I been fighting 'em my
            whole life.

                    ANGEL
        That creature's a vampire?

                         GUNN
            No, I never seen anything like that.

                         WESLEY
            (practically raising his hand)
            I have! OOh! It's a demon. Uh, probably of the
            Karathmamanyuhg family. See, some of us have as
            lightly broader base of exper —

                         GUNN
            How do you kill it?

                    WESLEY
        Well, I know this breed is, uh, nocturnal, and feeds
        on roots or possibly human effluvia, and, uh... it's a
        horned... race, as you see...

                         GUNN
            So you know jack.

> WESLEY
> They're nocturnal...

> GUNN
> I'm a get me one of those axes.

> WESLEY
> Hold on!

> GUNN
> Doesn't matter what it is! It looks wrong, it dies!

Wesley stands in his way and tries to push him back.

> WESLEY
> Not till we... find out...

Gunn gets him in a headlock, and the two continue struggling, neither with great panache.

> WESLEY (cont'd)
> Quit it!

> GUNN
> Get your... ow!

> WESLEY
> Watch the arms! Watch the arms!

ANGLE: CORDY AND ANGEL

> CORDELIA
> (to Angel)
> You gonna get in there and stop them?

> ANGEL
> (shakes his head)
> It's about time the English got what's coming to 'em.
> I'm rooting for the slave.

She just looks away.

ANGLE: LORNE is slumped in his chair as the two continue struggling in the background. He suddenly looks at camera:

> LORNE
> I know I'm unconscious during this part of the story,
> but can you believe these mooks? Champions of the
> world, ladies and gentlemen. Good thing that pert
> little Slayer's still kickin' around, am I right?

He goes back to being unconscious.

Cordy gets fed up, goes to the two and kicks them both in the shins really hard. They break apart.

> GUNN
> OW!

> WESLEY
> OW!

                    CORDELIA
          Enough! Okay? If Head Cheese here has a theory, then
          let's hear it —
          (Gunn moves to speak)

— BEFORE we go all Texas Chainsaw on deformo there.

Wes takes a moment to gloat at Gunn.

                    WESLEY
          There are stories at the Watcher's Academy of a
          test, a secret gauntlet that only the most cunning
          can survive. You're locked in a house with a vicious,
          deadly vampire, and you have to kill him, before he
          kills you. It's been done in the past with Slayers...

                    FRED
          Slayer? The band?

                    WESLEY
          No, it's... the point is, this may be a test. The
          weapons, the huge, mazelike locale, innocent civilians
          and a mysterious Karathmamanyuhg demon... this is a
          test.

                    FRED
          It's just like D&D! I can totally ace this! Is there
          dice?

                    GUNN
          I ain't a civilian. I been killin' vamps since I was
          twelve.

                    WESLEY
          Which only supports my theory. You must be here in an
          advisory capacity.

                    GUNN
          I think I'm here in a chop that green bitch's head off
          capacity and I don't give a damn about this "test".

                    FRED
          Are you always this grouchy?

                    GUNN
          Only when I wake up with a bunch of insane white folk
          telling me what to do. Day I take orders from guys
          like you is the... day I... not even gonna happen.

                    CORDELIA
          (to Wes)
          Keep explaining why we're not walking out that door.

                    ANGEL
          Because they did something to us.

Everyone looks at him.

                    ANGEL (cont'd)
          They changed us.

                    CORDELIA
          You mean this IS about my hair?

                    FRED
          I sorta see his point. Not one of y'all looks exactly
          seventeen.

They look at each other. It's true.

                    FRED (cont'd)
          It's like time has been pushed forward. Like we missed
          a bunch of years.

                    CORDELIA
          (looking down atherself)
          I kind of have filled out even more...

                    FRED
          (also looking down)
          And I apparently ain't gonna.

Wes feels a muscle — and is pleased as punch to actually find one there.

                    ANGEL
          I feel cold. Inside.

                    CORDELIA
          This is so unfair! I'm a craggy twenty something? What
          about the prom?

                    GUNN
          Could be that demon put a whammy on us. Could be he
          could take it back.

                    WESLEY
          (to Gunn)
          Well, he certainly couldn't with his head cut off,
          could he?

                    FRED
          So you think if we kill this vampire, they take off
          this spell whammy? We can go back to being ourselves?

                    CORDELIA
          And never see each other again?

                    WESLEY
          I believe we can all just go about our business.

                    CORDELIA
          And never see each other again?

                    GUNN
          Great. So we go vamp-hunting.

He heads to the weapons cabinet. Others follow, taking weapons as they talk:

                    GUNN (cont'd)
          This place looks pretty big. I say two groups.

                    CORDELIA
          (re: Angel)

> Great. I'm going with Tall, Dark and Slightly Less
> Pathetic Than You Two here. We'll try the rooms.

                    WESLEY
          And we'll look downstairs. If you find the vampire,
          remember he's a vicious animal. Just try to draw him
          towards us.

They split up. We follow Fred, Gunn and Wes.

                    WESLEY (cont'd)
          (to Fred)
          Don't worry. We'll win this day, I assure you.

                    FRED
          I'm ready, I'm okay. Be cooler if we could score some
          weed, though.

22 INT. ANGEL'S HOTEL - UPSTAIRS HALL - NIGHT

Cordy and Angel make their shmuch-baity way along the dark hall.

                    CORDELIA
          God, there's like a million rooms...

Angel stops, hearing the tinny drift of Cordy's radio. He turns to her, eyes
wide:

                    ANGEL
          Minstrels!

She gives him a look.

23 INT. ANGEL'S HOTEL - CORDY'S ROOM - NIGHT

They move slowly in. Angel picks up the radio, awed, until Cordy snaps it off.

                    ANGEL
          How did... you stopped the tiny men from singing.

He sits on the edge of the bed, overwhelmed. Cordy looks at him with some
sympathy, sits by him.

                    CORDELIA
          You really are far from home, aren't you?

                    ANGEL
          I tell you, I get through this, I'm going to have a
          great cup of ale — I don't care what father says it
          does to you.

She runs her hand along his back. They're falling into a slightly sexy vibe
here.

                    CORDELIA
          Maybe we should just sit tight. Let the vampire
          experts deal with this thing.

                    ANGEL
          I'm sorry for acting so womanish...

She holds his arms — yowsah! He's got muscles.

                    CORDELIA
          You're not... really not womanish.

                    ANGEL
          And you're very sweet.

                    CORDELIA
          (softly)
          You don't know the half of it...

She turns away a bit, still close to him...

                    CORDELIA (cont'd)
          What is it about danger that makes... makes your blood
          just...

His face is close to her neck — and he VAMPS. He leans in, pure hunger — she
looks back at him and he starts back, reverting.

                    CORDELIA (cont'd)
          What's wrong?

                    ANGEL
          Nothing. Excuse me.

He bolts into the bathroom —

24 INT. ANGEL'S HOTEL - CORDY'S BATHROOM - CONTINUING

— and looks in the mirror. Nothing looks back.

25 INT. ANGEL'S HOTEL - CORDY'S ROOM - CONTINUING

He comes back out, even more freaked.

                    ANGEL
          I'm invisible!

                    CORDELIA
          No you're not.

                    ANGEL
          Oh.
          (beat)
          Excuse me.

He goes back in and shuts the door.

26 INT. ANGEL'S HOTEL - CORDY' S BATHROOM - CONTINUING

Angel looks in the mirror again — nothing — then turns, feels his face. He
VAMPS, UNVAMPS. Again. Again. Faster.

27 INT. ANGEL'S HOTEL - CORDY' S ROOM - CONTINUING

Cordy is outside the bathroom as we hear the rhythmic squeak of Angel vamping
and unvamping rapidly.

                    CORDELIA
          What's going on?

ANGEL
(voice a panicky squeak)
I'm almost finished...

She looks puzzled.

28 INT. ANGEL'S HOTEL - CORDY'S BATHROOM - CONTINUING

Angel is back to regular face, and very much wigged out.

                    ANGEL
          (to himself)
          I'm a vampire.

He looks toward the door, fear dawning.

                    ANGEL (cont'd)
          They're gonna kill me...

                    END OF ACT TWO

                    ACT THREE

29 INT. CLUB - NIGHT

                         LORNE
          Well those were some exciting products, am I right?
          (claps along with audience) Let's all think about
          buying some of those. But if I can bring it down a
          moment... (the lights go blue and soft) Is there
          anything worse than feeling like you're all alone?

30 INT. ANGEL'S HOTEL - CORDY' S BEDROOM - NIGHT

As Lorne continues in V.O., Angel emerges from the bathroom, smiles weakly at
Cordy, and they head out again, Cordy a little confused.

                         LORNE (V.O.)
          Like you're the only person in the world who thinks
          the way you do, and if anyone else found out, they'd
          drive a pointy wooden thing through your heart? Yeah,
          we've all been there.

31 INT. CLUB - NIGHT

                         LORNE
          And as for our fearless vampire killers...

32 INT. ANGEL'S HOTEL - DOWNSTAIRS SPACE - NIGHT

(Or kitchen or other space, anything other than hallway would be nice.)

Gunn kicks a door open, stalks in with his battleaxe. Wes follows, very amateur
spy, then Fred, who's just thinking out loud.

                         FRED
          I just think we shouldn't be ruling out the idea of
          aliens. I mean, he is a greenish sort of fellah, and
          us bein' asleep all that time... I mean, think about
          it a minute.
          (Wes turns to her)
          All that time unconscious... they could've been doing
          heaven knows what. I can just see myself... lying on
          a table, no clothes, no will, while they probed and
          explored and did whatever they wanted to my naked
          helpless body.

Wesley's wooden stake pops involuntarily from his sleeve. He rushes to push it back in.

                    FRED (cont'd)
          It's horrible.

                    WESLEY
          Horrible, yes. But I assure you, this is demonic work,
          and they're not... so exploratory as... don't be
          afraid.

He reaches out to touch her hair, comfortingly, as Gunn reappears and Wes snaps back to business.

>   GUNN
> Ain't nothing here. This is getting old.

>   WESLEY
> Well, let's not give up probe. Hope. Give up hope. We
> not.

They exit.

33 INT. ANGEL'S HOTEL - LOBBY - NIGHT

Lorne is still out. The three are waiting as the two come down stairs.

>   WESLEY
> Any luck?

>   ANGEL
> We saw no vampires of any kind anywhere.

>   WESLEY
> Did you check all the rooms?

>   CORDELIA
> Only the ones that wanted turn down service. There's
> five floors! My feet hurt. You finish.

>   GUNN
> This is a waste of time.

>   ANGEL
> I agree. There's nothing here. This place is evil and
> I think I should leave now. Because of the evil.

He moves quickly to the door.

>   WESLEY
> Don't be a fool!

>   ANGEL
> Good luck, all!

He exits out the front. Beat.

>   GUNN
> So we're all locked in, huh?

>   CORDELIA
> Excuse me, did I just get the brush off? Did a guy
> just bail on me? There really is some kind of horrible
> spell.

She plops herself down on the poof.

>   FRED
> Do you think Liam's okay out there?

>   GUNN
> If something's eatin' him, at least he ain't as bored
> as me.

> WESLEY
>
> Joke all you like. Liam right now may well be facing horrors he's never even imagined.

34 EXT. STREET OUTSIDE HOTEL - CONTINUING

CLOSE ON: ANGEL

Facing horrors he's never even imagined. Camera comes around to find that what he's facing is traffic. Cars and trucks whiz by, impossibly loud.

A moment, and Angel turns tail and runs.

35 INT. ANGEL'S HOTEL - LOBBY - MOMENTS LATER

Angel rushes in, slamming the door behind him, and up against it in terror.

> FRED
>
> Liam!

> ANGEL
>
> Demons...

> WESLEY
> (scared)
> Really?
> (smug, to Gunn)
> Told you.
> (scared)
> How many?

> ANGEL
>
> Hundreds. Screaming.

He moves suddenly from the door, as if they might burst through.

> FRED
>
> Will they try to get in?

> ANGEL
>
> I don't think they saw me.

> FRED
>
> I guess we really better solve this puzzle and all.

As Angel passes Wes:

> WESLEY
>
> What type of demon, would you say?

> ANGEL
>
> Shiny.

Wes considers this as Angel sits by Cordy, a gesture she of course assumes is about her.

> CORDELIA
> (to herself)
> Yep. Still got it.

> GUNN
>
> So that means we gotta check the rest of the rooms? Cause I'm bored just sayin' it.

CORDELIA
I second the motion to be really bored.

Angel finds himself staring at her neck again.

FRED
Wouldn't the vampire be coming after us anyhow? Aren't
we vittles?

WESLEY
And he should be starving, by rule. But I also happen
to think further searching would be pointless. I think
the council has been cleverer than I imagined.

FRED
Ooh! How?

                          GUNN
             (bored sarcasm)
          Yeah, speech, speech.

                          WESLEY
          Five people. Each unknown to each other, far from
          home, trapped together at night. I submit that the
          bloodsucking fiend may be even closer than we dared
          suspect. That it may be-

                          ANGEL
             (standing)
          I'll search the rooms.

                          WESLEY
          I was getting to the good part!

                          ANGEL
             (starts to go)
          But we can't just wait for the vampire to appear, I'll
          just flush him out and—

                          WESLEY
          That it may be one of us!

Angel stops, turns back. All eyes are on Wes.

                          CORDELIA
          You're kidding.

                          WESLEY
          Would that I were, Miss Chase.
             (looking at Angel)
          But the simple fact is, the fiend has been right under
          our noses the entire time, waiting for the moment to
          STRIKE!

And on that word he whips out a cross and holds it right up to the face of
Gunn.

Beat.

Gunn pops Wes in the nose.

                          WESLEY (cont'd)
          D-ah-ooh.

                          ANGEL
          See? The English is stupid. Let's have a different
          theory.

                          WESLEY
             (holding his nose)
          I'm not quite finished. I think it's only fair that
          every one has a turn. The cross obviously doesn't
          affect me, or our friend the pugilist...

                          GUNN
          Your ass better pray I don't look that word up.

Cordy stands, takes the cross. Nothing. Bored. Angel waits with growing unease
as she hands it to Fred, who runs it over herself like an airport scanner.

She turns to Angel. He smiles blandly. She hands him the cross.

CLOSE ON: His hand, closing around it. We hear a slight sizzling sound..

> ANGEL
> See. No vampires here. I'm just like all of you.

A bit of smoke begins to rise from his hand. The sizzling continues.

> FRED
> Does anyone else hear-

> ANGEL
> Look! The devil's awake!

The all look. Lorne is, in fact, coming to.

They move to him as Angel tosses the cross away behind him, shaking his hand in pain.

> LORNE
> Whoah...

> WESLEY
> Don't get too close...

> LORNE
> (focusing)
> Guys! Hey! That was quite a whammy. A little trip through the transitive nightfall of diamonds, if you know what I mean, and I certainly don't.

> ANGEL
> He speaks madness.

> LORNE
> Here's a funny sidebar: I'm tied to a chair. AGAIN. What the Hell's going on?

> WESLEY
> We were hoping you would enlighten us, spawn of evil.

> LORNE
> Oh dear, Starting to suspect my "surefire hit" spell closed out of town, hrnnnn... did anything go right? Did Cordy at least get her memory back?

> CORDELIA
> There's nothing wrong with my memory and where do you get off calling me "Cordy" like we're buddies?

> LORNE
> Look, kiddies, why don't we untie uncle Lorne and I can set this all-

> WESLEY
> Just tell us where the vampire is, fiend.

> LORNE
> What are you talking about? There aren't any vampires here.

Angel breathes a sigh of relief.

>   LORNE (cont'd)
>   (pointing)
>   I mean, besides our boy here.

They all look at Angel. He fumbles to cover:

>   ANGEL
>   Lying devil-man!

>   LORNE
>   (oh come on)
>   Oh, what, the spell made you not a vampire anymore? My
>   magic isn't that-

>   ANGEL
>   Shut your mouth!

And he hits Lorne. Lorne goes flying back abnormally far in his chair - in mid-flight we cut to:

36 INT. CLUB - NIGHT

Lorne just looks at the camera a moment. In a complaining tone:

>   LORNE
>   Ow...

37 INT. ANGEL'S HOTEL - LOBBY - NIGHT

Lorne's chair finishes its flight, landing with Lorne on his back, briefly out again.

Angel looks at his fist - wow, strong. He looks at everyone else as they eye him with suspicion and fear.

>   ANGEL
>   It's not... He just...

>   WESLEY
>   Well. A mystery solved.

>   GUNN
>   Explains the lame-ass cover story about being Irish,
>   too.

Gunn, with his axe, and Wes start circling Angel as the girls back off a bit.

>   CORDELIA
>   Is this a convenient time to point out that you left
>   me alone with him, genius?
>   (off Wes's look)
>   You'll let me know.

>   ANGEL
>   Well, I never touched her.

>   CORDELIA
>   So clearly, deviant.

                    ANGEL
          I'm not!

Over his next line, Wes shakes his arm to get his stake to pop out, which it
eventually does.

                    WESLEY
          Vampires are all... the... same, my friend. There's
          nothing human in them.

                    GUNN
          Man's right. You ain't a person. Just dust waitin' to
          happen.

                    ANGEL
          I don't want to hurt anyone...

                    FRED
          What do we do?

She is beside Wes - he feels her presence...

                    WESLEY
          Don't fear. It's under control...

She touches his shoulder, saying:

                    FRED
          But are you sure we should-

And of course a moment after she touches him, his stake flies out and embeds
itself in Angel's mid flank.

                    ANGEL
          (doubling over)
          AAH!

                    WESLEY
          Sorry! I mean, hah!

Angel looks back up at him - in VAMP FACE. Pulls out the stake. Everyone starts
back except Gunn, who slices from behind - and cuts Angel's back. Angel screams,
spins and grabs Gunn's throat, throws him far against a wall. Gunn's out.

Cordy ducks down behind the poof. Wes steps fully in front of Fred, actually
managing to get his sword out with some aplomb.

                    ANGEL
          You want a vampire, then? I guess I'm your man! I
          guess I'll be feeding on your corpses. Starting with
          the girls. And don't think you'll escape notice,
          hiding behind that poof.

                    WESLEY
          Now see here - oh. Her.

                    ANGEL
          No, you. So, who'd like to be the first course? Hard
          to choose between you girls.

                          CORDELIA
                    (standing)
               What do you mean, it's hard?
                    (oops)
               I mean, she's the tasty one! Look at her! Half of her
               is neck!

                          WESLEY
               Miss Chase, Miss Burkle... run.

He charges Angel, swinging. Cordy runs down the hall, Fred ducks into the
office.

Wes swipes at Angel, who dodges - without the grace he's famous for. He gets
inside the blade and elbows Wes in the face. Wes goes down but not out.

Angel looks where Cordy ran, more resentment than hunger in his eyes, and runs
after her.

38 INT. ANGEL'S HOTEL - DOWNSTAIRS SPACE - NIGHT

The same place Wes, Fred and Gunn came before. Cordy runs in, finds it's a dead
end. She hides, waiting in terror. Angel enters (no longer in vampface), stops.

                          ANGEL
               It baffles me. You liked me so much before... now I
               can't even get a little kiss?

He turns, looks into the shadows where she is.

                          ANGEL (cont'd)
               I can see you. Hell, woman, I can smell you. Are you
               really set to playing these games?

She bolts for the entrance - he grabs her, playfully holds her.

                          ANGEL (cont'd)
               I seem to be strong, too, and fast. It's not so bad,
               this vampire thing.

                          CORDELIA
               Well, I got a super power of my own, hotshot.

                          ANGEL
               And what's that now.

She emits an EAR-SPLITTING SCREAM. He actually winces, lets go a bit. But she
runs out of breath and he's still got her by the wrist.

                          ANGEL (cont'd)
               That really is inhuman. But what good do you think
               it's gonna —

And CONNOR SLAMS into him, takes him to the ground. Angel throws him off and
they come up, both nearly snarling.

Wes comes running after, calling out:

                          WESLEY
               Yes, that's the one! Kill that one, please!

                    CONNOR
          You're never gonna touch her again.

                    CORDELIA
          (to Connor)
          I think I love you.

Connor is actually thrown by this — he looks at Cordy — and Angel rushes him.
But he still has his skills, he easily uses Angel's momentum to spin him and
hurl him through a window...

39 INT. ANGEL'S HOTEL - KITCHEN - CONTINUING

...where Angel flies down onto a landing and thence to the ground. Lands hard
and badly, groaning.

40 INT. ANGEL'S HOTEL - DOWNSTAIRS SPACE - CONTINUING

Cordy runs to Connor, clings to him not unlike the Whore did.

                    CORDY
          Thank you thank you thank you.

                    CONNOR
          Why did he attack you?

                    CORDY
          Who wouldn't? Look, you're a wee bit chess club for my
          usual beat, but you kill that freak and you're getting
          a BIG reward.

                    CONNOR
          You mean that?

                    CORDY
          Hoo doggy.

Off Connor, looking toward the window...

                    END OF ACT THREE

                    ACT FOUR

41 INT. ANGEL'S HOTEL - KITCHEN - NIGHT

ANGLE on the ground as Connor's feet land right where Angel had fallen. Connor
moves slowly about in shadow, listening — and easily ducks when Angel comes from
the shadows swinging. Connor sweeps him low, tripping him up and sending him
onto his back. Connor jumps on him, but Angel grabs his arm, gets in close
wrestler-style, pushing him back up and against the counter, twisting Connor's
arm til he nearly screams.

                    ANGEL
          I'm a bit tired of being bullied.

Connor gets in a shot, they trade, close, and Connor hurls Angel over the counter.
Angel rises and they jockey for position, neither with a shot at the other.

42 INT. ANGEL'S HOTEL - LOBBY - NIGHT

Fred peeps out from her hiding place. She runs to check on Gunn, who groans,
still out of it. But Lorne, nearby, is wide awake now.

                         LORNE
          Uh, sweetie?

                         FRED
          Ahh!

                         LORNE
          If I can take a minute of your time, we have a huge
          problem. But I can solve it.

                         FRED
          Why should I trust you?

                         LORNE
          'Cause we're buddies, Freddikins! We did a spell, it
          went wrong — I'll be getting a big incorporeal refund,
          tell you right now, but we can make it right! Is the
          bottle still there? On the floor, in the circle.

She looks.

                         FRED
          You mean those bitty bits of broken glass?

                         LORNE
          Oh, balls. Well, we can still do it, maybe one at a
          time. You just gotta untie me first.

                         FRED
          I don't know...

                         LORNE
          Look into your heart, Fred. Am I evil?

A moment, and she gets a sword to cut him loose. Stops.

                         FRED
          You promise you're not some alien that's been secretly
          probing me?

                         LORNE
          No, honey, we're just good friends.

43 INT. ANGEL'S HOTEL - KITCHEN - NIGHT

Angel and Connor are still squared off.

                         ANGEL
          You're stronger than the rest. Are you not a Vampire
          yourself then?

                         CONNOR
          You don't remember.

                         ANGEL
          I remember waking up here, in this madhouse with that
          fine lot of hypocties...

                         CONNOR
          Hypocrites.

                    ANGEL
          I'm supposed to be evil, but they attack me without
          cause. Gang up on me 'cause I'm different. They're as
          bad as my father.

                    CONNOR
          (slyly)
          Fathers. Don't they suck?

                    ANGEL
          Say one thing, then... "Be good, fear God, do as
          you're told..." all the while I know good and well
          he's had his share of sinning.

                    CONNOR
          Sounds kinda like my dad.

                    ANGEL
          Is he a self-righteous bastard?

                    CONNOR
          You'd be amazed.

Connor LEAPS over the rack atop the counter — but Angel dives UNDER the rack and
they both end up on the opposite side again.

                    CONNOR (cont'd)
          You afraid to fight me?

                    ANGEL
          Truth to tell, I'm not much for fighting. I'd rather
          be satisfying my sinful urges with the Chase girl.

                    CONNOR
          You keep the hell away from her.

                    ANGEL
          Oh, the girl's yours, then?

                    CONNOR(hesitates)
          That's right.

                    ANGEL
          She never did mention you when we were alone togeth —

Talking too much. Connor whips a pan lid at him, nails him in the face.
Before Angel can recover, Connor grabs the rack and slides feet-first across
the counter, nailing Angel in the chest.

44 INT. ANGEL'S HOTEL - LOBBY - NIGHT

Fred closes her eyes and sticks out her tongue. Reverse to see Lorne with a
pestle, looking uncertainly into it.

                    FRED (tongue still out)
          Huwwy uh, I'm nuhvous.

He sticks his finger in the paste in the pestle and then dabs it on her tongue.
She swallows, makes a lemon face, then staggers back in revelation.

                    FRED (cont'd)
          Oh, lord.

138

LORNE
Did it work?

Before she can answer, Gunn rises up behind Lorne with his axe, about to swing —

FRED
WAIT!

45 INT. ANGEL'S HOTEL - KITCHEN - NIGHT

Angel and Connor are beating the shit out of each other. It's Massalicious. Eventually, despite Connor's finesse, Angel's relentless strength wears him down. He lands Connor on the floor, stands over him.

CONNOR
Happy now?

ANGEL
I didn't ask for this. I didn't ask to be attacked. I didn't ask to be a freak.

He starts to walk away, sullen.

ANGEL (cont'd)
Hell, I didn't ask to be born.

Something like sympathy crosses Connor's face. He rises.

CONNOR
Wait.

ANGEL
What do you want? Another beating?

CONNOR
I SO almost had you.

ANGEL
Not in a dream!

Fred pops her head through the upper window:

FRED
Hold it! Nobody kill anybody; Please.

46 INT. ANGEL'S HOTEL - LOBBY - NIGHT

Wes retrieves his stake, as Gunn and Fred clean up other things. Neither says a word.

LORNE (V.O.)
So, all's well that ends well, right kiddies?

Wes exits, passing Fred, who is busy smelling something strange and icky in one of the ferns. A simple, mournful piano tune has begun.

47 INT. ANGEL'S HOTEL - HALL OUTSIDE CORDY'S ROOM - NIGHT

Cordy gets a daub from Lorne on her tongue. Swallows — and her eyes go wide. She looks over at Angel and Connor, both looking awkward, and she turns on her tail and goes, unable to cope (Slo-mo).

>   LORNE (V.O.)
>   But since nothing ended all that well, I guess I gotta
>   say that well, nothing WAS well.

48 INT. CLUB - NIGHT

We see that it's Lome himself playing the piano (hands hidden) as he talks.

>   LORNE
>   See, none of us knew it then, but the sequence of
>   events was a little different than we thought. It went
>   more like this:

49 INT. ANGEL'S HOTEL - HALL OUTSIDE CORDY'S ROOM - NIGHT

The same moment, Cordy getting her taste, then:

50 INT. BLACK UNDERBELLY OF HELL - NIGHT

We see a pair of unutterably evil, glowing eyes snap open to a huge musical sting.

CUT BACK TO:

51 INT. ANGEL'S HOTEL - HALL OUTSIDE CORDY' S ROOM - NIGHT

The same shot of Cordy bailing.

52 INT. CLUB - NIGHT

Lorne looks down at the keys. (The theme may still be playing, even though he's not.)

>   LORNE
>   I like to think this wasn't all my fault. That she
>   would have gotten her memory back somehow - maybe
>   without all the wacky hi-jinks we've all enjoyed so
>   much... and that everything that happened would have
>   happened anyway. But I also like to think Patti
>   LaBelle secretly wants to be my best friend, so me and
>   reality... Well. It's been a long night. For everyone.
>   Hope you all enjoyed my little tale so much you tip
>   your waitresses with obnoxious abandon.

>   OFFSCREEN MAN
>   Finish it!

>   LORNE
>   (Rising)
>   Always leave 'em wanting more, kiddo, that's the rule.
>   Anyway, there's no more to tell. Applause applause...
>   I gotta sea breeze that's gonna up and leave with
>   someone else if I don't get to her soon. You kids be
>   good.. Go home, hug your families while you can. Stay
>   away from the magic. Trust me.

His jacket is off, and he takes it from off the piano...

53 INT. ANGEL'S HOTEL - HALLWAY - NIGHT

Cordy is leaving, truly freaked out. Angel catches up with her.

>   ANGEL
>   Cordy.

She stop, turns.

>   CORDY
>   I can't. Angel, I'm sorry...

>   ANGEL
>   You remember?

>   CORDY
>   I remember all of it. All of it. And I have to be
>   alone. Please. For a while. It's too...

She starts to go again.

>   ANGEL
>   Cordelia.

She waits.

>   ANGEL (cont'd)
>   Were we in love?

She turns back to him.

>   CORDY
>   We were.

And she leaves. He watches her go.

54 INT. CLUB - NIGHT

Lorne finishes putting on his jacket and heads off stage. Although we can still hear the ambient crowd noise we now see for the first time that it is empty.

Lorne walks off between the tables, into the light of morning,

<u>THE END</u>

ANGEL
"Spin the Bottle"

SET LIST INTERIORS

CLUB

ANGEL'S HOTEL
     COURTYARD
     FREAD AND GUNN'S ROOM
     LOBBY
     CORDY'S ROOM
     OFFICE
     GARDEN
     UPSTAIRS HALL
     CORDY'S BATHROOM
     CORDY'S BEDROOM
     DOWNSTAIRS SPACE (or kitchenor other space)
     KITCHEN
     HALL OUTSIDE CORDY'S ROOM
     HALLWAY

WESLEY'S APARTMENT

BLACK UNDERBELLY OF HELL

EXTERIORS

STREET - NIGHT

ALLEY - NIGHT

STREET OUTISDE HOTEL - NIGHT

ANGEL

issue four

scriptbook ™

Episode
WAITING IN THE WINGS

Written By
JOSS WHEDON

ANGEL™
"WAITING IN THE WINGS"

WRITTEN BY

JOSS WHEDON

Starring:
DAVID BOREANAZ
CHARISMA CARPENTER
ALEXIS DENISOF
J. AUGUST RICHARDS
AMY ACKER
ANDY HALLETT
RODNEY PECK
MARK HARELIK
DON TIFFANY
SUMMER GLAU
MARK LUTZ

Created By
JOSS WHEDON
&
DAVID GREENWALT

Written and Directed By
JOSS WHEDON

1 INT. HOTEL LOBBY/GARDEN - MORNING

ANGLE ON: An engraving of a hideous female (i.e. Six-breasted) demon with a human limb in its mouth. It's all gross.

>   WESLEY (O.S.)
>   Beautiful...

Widen to see WESLEY going through a demon book with a dreamy look on his face.

>   WESLEY
>   Honestly, have you ever seen anything lovelier? So
>   graceful, so... full of life... and those eyes... make
>   you feel like you're the only man in the room.

CORDELIA looks over his shoulder.

>   CORDELIA
>   Pius, six breasts -- any guy's gotta love that.

>   WESLEY
>   (confused)
>   Fred doesn't have six breasts.
>   (suddenly worried)
>   Right?

>   CORDELIA
>   (indicating picture)
>   Sorialus the Ravager. And, yeah, she's the one from my
>   vision.

>   WESLEY
>   Coming to destroy the humans that killed her mate.

>   CORDELIA
>   But not for another month or so. I'll file her under
>   pending. You gonna ask her out?

>   WESLEY
>   The Ravager?

>   CORDELIA
>   Fred.

>   WESLEY
>   Oh. Yes. Yes. But you know, timing. I'll make my move
>   right when I feel the iron is hot.

>   CORDELIA
>   Well, get it done, Johnnie Reb, so I can hear about
>   something else and you can do something besides
>   feeling your hot iron.

>   WESLEY
>   Am I very boring on the subject?

                              CORDELIA
                    (playful)
                    You know, there was a time when you thought I was the
                    loveliest thing in the world.

                              WESLEY
                    Well, I... you're an extraordinary woman, and certain-
                    ly beautiful, I --

                              CORDELIA
                    At ease, soldier. Just like to head it every now and
                    then. Get a little of the love. Something, anyway. I
                    was the ditsiest bitch in Sunnydale, coulda had any
                    man I wanted; now I'm all superhero-y and the best
                    action I can get is an invisible ghost who's good with
                    a loofah.

She realizes she's shared too much. Wesley smiles sympathetically.

                              WESLEY
                    I'm sorry, I missed that last part.

                              CORDELIA
                    You are a gentleman.

                              ANGEL
                    Who's doing what with a loofah?

Of course he's right there, and of course he missed the point entirely.

                              WESLEY
                    Not loofah... Loo... FAHnoocthskmuh. Demon: very...
                    cleansing, bad demon --

                              CORDELIA
                    So! What's up with you? Hey, you went with the dark
                    colors today! It's a look.

Angel smiles.

                              ANGEL
                    Ask me why I'm smiling.

                              CORDELIA
                    I will because it's scaring me.

Angel reaches into his pocket, pulls out five tickets to something.

                              ANGEL
                    We... are steppin' out.

ANGLE: IN THE GARDEN FRED and GUNN are walking together, arriving from breakfast.

(Note: If the walk and talk times out long, I will want to double side the
set dressing beyond the gate and shoot some of this on their backs before they
reach it.)

                              GUNN
                    So as soon as the restaurant closed, BAM, I jimmy it
                    and we're in there eating everything. Alonna's cookin'
                    up steaks, I'm pulling out bottles of wine -- 'cause

it's hard to find a wine that goes with every single
item of food in the place, which is pretty much what
we ate. There wasn't any "Think ahead. Save it for
later", just the moment: us living high.

He pauses, remembering. Fred worries:

> FRED
> I'm sorry if, you... I didn't mean to bring up your
> sister...

> GUNN
> No, I like talking about her. With you, anyway. You
> kind of remind me of her.

Fred is clearly affected by the compliment.

> GUNN (cont'd)
> Particularly the way you can shovel a mountain range
> of food into your mouth, that is some Olympian feat,
> that much eating --

> FRED
> Oh, was I a pig? It's just that first breakfast seems
> to go so quick and I'm always still --

> GUNN
> I'm just wondering where it goes in that little stick-
> figure body you got.

She hits him, offended.

> FRED
> Stick -- you're a beast.

> GUNN
> Oh, come on, you know you're gorgeous.

He's through the doors as he says it, not even realizing the effect THAT compliment has on her. She follows in after a moment.

> GUNN (cont'd)
> Morning, friends and neighbors.

Helios from the three as Gunn sees on the counter:

> GUNN (cont'd)
> Are those the tickets? You got ' em?

> ANGEL (excited)
> Well I got to the ticket place and --

> GUNN
> Oh, I'm paying you back. This is on me.

> WESLEY
> Good morning, Fred.

> FRED
> Hey.

She crosses to Wes as Gunn approaches the tix.

>   FRED (cont'd)
>   Did you find out the scary?

>   WESLEY
>   Eventually -- do you want to see?

>   FRED
>   Yeah yeah!

>   GUNN
>   Mahta Hari is the tightest band in L.A., you guys are
>   gonna be tripping out --

>   ANGEL
>   The only thing is --

>   GUNN
>   I said I'm good for it, man -- don't have to worry
>   about dipping into Connor's college fund. Time I saw
>   Mahta Hari at the Troubador, they were the Blinnikov
>   World Ballet Corps...

He's reading that last part, slower, his expression changing.

>   GUNN (cont'd)
>   What's going on?

>   ANGEL
>   Trying to tell you. I went to the ticket place and
>   Boom. Tonight only.

>   GUNN
>   But... you got ballet on my Mahta Hari tickets.

>   ANGEL
>   This is the Blinnikov World Ballet Corps.

>   CORDELIA
>   He's been saying that like it has meaning.

>   ANGEL
>   This is one of the premiere companies in the world.
>   And they're doing Giselle! It's their signature piece.

>   GUNN
>   This is all like some horrible dream.

>   WESLEY
>   I think I've heard of them -- very ahead of their
>   time.

>   ANGEL
>   Oh yeah. I saw their production of Giselle in 1890 --
>   cried like a baby. And I was evil!

>   FRED
>   I think it sounds exciting.

                    WESLEY
          Yes, yes.

                    GUNN
          No, no...

                    ANGEL
          Gunn.

                    GUNN
          (more desperate than angry)
          This is not Mahta Hari. This is tutus, and the guys
          with their big-ass packages jumping up and down...
          this is just...
          (to Angel)
          I will never trust you again. The trust is gone.

                    CORDELIA
          Oh, get over it.
          (to Angel)
          Do we get dressed up?

                    ANGEL
          Of course.

                    CORDELIA
          I'm in.

                    ANGEL
          (to all)
          Seeing real ballet, live, it's... it's like another
          world.

                    ANGEL
          (to Gunn)
          Gunn, these guys are tight, and you're gonna be trip-
          ping out.

                    GUNN
          Don't be using my own phrases when we've lost the
          trust.

                    CORDELIA
          Come on. Guys, working day. Cases to solve.

Everyone fades toward the office as Gunn continues to hold the tickets, lost.

                    GUNN
          Okay, but, I'm not still paying, right, 'cause... it's
          like a nightmare...

2 INT. BOX SEAT, THEATRE - DAY

A THEATER MANAGER is showing the box to THE COUNT. The house lights are not up,
and it's dark and elegantly atmospheric in here. The Count appears to be a man
out of time, he is so elegantly dressed, he wears what looks like a royal medal,
a bejewelled affair on a ribbon around his neck. He observes the box, looks to
the stage.

                    MANAGER
          I hope this box is all right.

The count says nothing.

                    MANAGER (cont'd)
          It's such an honor to have the company here,
          I have to say. All of L.A. is buzzing. To
          have the Blinnikov performing
          Giselle... I can't imagine what
          tonight's going to be like.

                    THE COUNT
          It will be the performance of a
          lifetime.

He smiles wanly to the little sycophant. Turns and looks
to the stage and something cold flashes in his eyes.

                    THE COUNT
          I guarantee it.

                    END OF TEASER

3 INT. FANCY CLOTHING STORE - DAY

Fred and Cordy are shopping together. The place is wicked
fancy -- Cordy's right at home, but Fred not so much.

                    FRED
          Are you certain this is the right
          place for us?

                    CORDELIA
          Well, we could get our
          outfits at Cavegirl's
          House of Burlap, but
          that's just so last
          season. The boys are
          all renting tuxes, we
          gotta step up.

She holds a dress up against Fred.
Considers.

                    FRED
          But aren't we, you know...
          poor?

She puts the dress back, keeps looking.

                    CORDELIA
          There is an old custom amongst my people. It's called
          buying a dress, wearing it once, and returning it the
          next day. It's all about hiding the tags while it's on.

                    FRED
          Ohhhh! Okay. I'm very excited about tonight. I love
          ballet. I mean, I haven't seen that much but my family
          went to the Nutcracker every Christmas and I had my
          first sexual dream about the Mouse King.
          (beat)
          I often could shut up more.

> CORDELIA
> It's overrated.

> FRED
> The Nutcracker?

> CORDELIA
> Shutting up. Face me.

She holds another dress up. Nope.

> FRED
> Can I ask you a question?

> CORDELIA
> I think you guys are perfect for each other.
> (off her look)
> I have magic powers, remember?

> FRED
> It's not like we've said anything... He's just so
> sweet, and commanding, and I feel so comfortable
> around him... I mean, I don't even know if he feels --

> CORDELIA
> He feels.

> FRED
> He feels? Feelings?

> CORDELIA
> There's definite feelings. We find you the right
> outfit for tonight, there may be actual feeling.

Fred is made of smile.

> FRED
> And then we gotta find a dress for you. Something
> that'll make Angel crazy.

> CORDELIA
> Fred, sweetie, Angel IS crazy.

> FRED
> Well, I know he'll wanna look his best for you...

> CORDELIA
> That's right. The world's champion is gonna spend all
> day worrying about his outfit.

4 INT. ANGEL'S HOTEL - ANGEL'S BEDROOM - NIGHT

Angel is looking over his shoulder, standing stiffly, worried.

> ANGEL
> Is it gonna be all right? Is there a stain?

We see Lorne pop up behind him --

> LORNE
> Relax, crumbcake. I got this soda water working
> overtime.

We see now that Host is cleaning a stain on the back of Angel's jacket.

> LORNE (cont'd)
> Man, that little Connor burps like a champ. Mickey
> Mantle smacking this bit of stewed apricot into the
> cheap seats.

> ANGEL
> At least he's sleeping.

> LORNE
> (finishes)
> Who wouldn't, that sweet Irish lullaby you crooned,
> just a hair flat on the bridge but more to the point,
> Cordelia?

> ANGEL
> What about her?

> LORNE
> I read you while you were singing, you big corn muf-
> fin. And I can't say as I blame, I mean what a woman
> she's become.

> ANGEL
> You're not supposed to read me and anyway you read me
> wrong.

> LORNE
> Sorry, Strudel, but it's not just when you're singing.
> There's a little term we had on Pylea, "Kyrumption" --

> ANGEL
> I know it.

> LORNE
> Okay! When two great heroes come together --

> ANGEL
> There's no coming together. Okay? Everything we've
> been through, and all anyone wants to talk about --

> LORNE
> Can't fight Kyrumption, cinnamon buns. It's fate, it's
> the stars, kyrumption --

> ANGEL
> Stop saying that! And stop calling me pastries.

The Host pauses, gets serious.

> LORNE
> You're a man of many limitations, Angel. Can't go out
> in the sun, can't feel the fresh air fill your lungs,
> can't, uh, achieve a certain level of physical intimacy
> without turning apocalyptically evil. But you're a
> man. You got a heart. It may not keep time but it's in
> there. And Cordelia is a hell of a lady. If I thought
> she liked to wear green I'd be elbowing you out of the
> way. But she's out of my league. She's a champion.
> Angel. Old school. Besides, we all know you got a
> thing for ex-cheerleaders.

Angel says nothing. Until:

                    ANGEL
          What have I got to offer her?

                    LORNE
          Do I even have to answer that? You just gotta act.
          Angel. Gotta let her know what's brewing inside 'cause
          man, it's real, and you don't wanna miss that shot.

                    ANGEL
          Lorne, Cordelia, she's....

                    CORDELIA
          She's what?

She is standing at the door. Stunning doesn't cover it. The boys are agape.

                    CORDELIA (cont'd)
          I'm waiting...

                    ANGEL
          I was jut saying you're... not a ballet fan.

                    LORNE
          (aside to Angel)
     You know, disregard everything I said. I forgot how
     homely she was, Hnnnhn...

                    ANGEL
          (to Cordy)
     You, uh... look... like...

                    CORDELIA
          (entering)
     A ballet fan. An aficionado -- a devotee, in fact.
     Tonight, I've decided we don't have to be our
     incredibly dreary selves.

She fixes Angel's tie absently as she talks.

                    CORDELIA (cont'd)
     Tonight, we're just a couple of young sophisticates
     enjoying an evening of classical dance. How does that
     sound?

Angel cannot help but smile.

                    ANGEL
     That sounds just right.

                    CORDELIA
     How's our boy?

                    ANGEL
     Fast asleep.

                    LORNE
     And I'll make sure he stays that way. He so much as
     peeps, I'll chloroform him.

Angel and Cordy throw him a look.

                    LORNE (cont'd)
     New parents. Never with the humor.

5 INT. ANGEL'S HOTEL - LOBBY - NIGHT

Fred is standing in the middle of the room, waiting. We see her in close-up: she
is more done-up than usual.

                    GUNN (O.S.)
     You gotta promise not to laugh.

                    FRED
     I promise.

                    GUNN (O.S.)
     It's gotta come from the heart.

                    FRED
     Will you stop being such a little girl? I promise.

Gunn steps out of the office in his tux. He is James Fucking Bond. Born to wear
a tux. He looks uncomfortable, but stops when he sees:

                                                                        155

ANGLE: FRED

In her dress. It's very different from Cordy's, but every inch as alluring. She is staring at Gunn, blown away by the look.

Then, surprisingly, she laughs.

> GUNN
> So this is what your promises are worth. I'm having a lot of trust issues at this time in my life.

> FRED
> (stopping)
> I'm sorry, it's just... My God, you're so pretty!

He smiles, the compliment settling on him as softly as the suit.

> GUNN
> You know there's not a lot of people could say that to me and live. But the way you look, there's no way I can fight you.

> FRED
> Tonight feels... I don't know, kind of magical. Is that stupid?

Wesley appears suddenly in frame, coming up behind Fred and draping a coat around her shoulders. He's dressed as well and we are five for five, people, hotties all round. He passes Fred a bit to look at Gunn.

> WESLEY
> Not at all.
> (to Gunn)
> Finally come out of hiding.

> GUNN
> And look at my reward.

Wesley turns to look at Fred.

> WESLEY
> Yes. Isn't she a vision.

Gunn looks up at the stairs.

> GUNN
> Lotta that going around.

ANGLE ON: Angel and Cordy coming down the stairs, arms linked. They practically float.

> CORDELIA
> Thank you, no thank you. There will be no visions tonight.

> ANGEL
> How can you be sure?

> CORDELIA
> I had a vision.

He doesn't try to unriddle it, just lets the collective good mood carry him as they head for the front door.

As they walk, Cordy whispers in Wesley's ear:

> CORDELIA (cont'd)
> The iron is hot.

He looks at her and she nods, sagely, sure. He smiles and moves on.

6 EXT. THEATRE - NIGHT

We push in, Limo POV, at the magnificent (good luck, guys) theatre. Well dressed patrons entering.

7 INT. AUDITORIUM/STAGE - NIGHT

ANGLE ON: Our gang, getting into their seats. Gunn, Fred and Wes are in the row directly in front of Angel and Cordy. The seats are pretty far back.

> ANGEL
> Sorry they're not closer -- getting five seats
> together was --

> WESLEY
> Don't be silly. Best place. Get the whole panorama
> from here.

> CORDELIA
> Besides, back here we stand less chance of setting off
> the "Under 70" alarm.

The lights begin to dim...

> ANGEL
> Back in the day, I'd always get box seats... or eat
> the people who had 'em.

> CORDELIA
> Don't let's reminisce. We're here. Enjoy.

8 INT. BOX SEAT, THEATRE - CONTINUING

The lights continue to dim as we see the Count settle into place, intent on the stage.

ANGLE: THE STAGE

As the curtain rises and the dance begins. We hold on the dance for a while, then HARD CUT TO:

9 INT. AUDITORIUM/STAGE - LATER

Cordelia SNORES in foreground, head back, mouth open. Looking as unglamorous as possible. Angel watches the ballet, looks over at her, looks around a bit -- her snoring is audible to others. Finally he adjusts his position, subtly nudging her. Instead of waking up, she just snuggles into his shoulder. Contentedly, he goes back to watching.

We pull past Wes and Fred to reveal Gunn, who is just enraptured, watching the dance almost like it was a great sports event -- he has to keep from cheering.

ANGLE: ON STAGE

The dance continues.

10 INT. AUDITORIUM/STAGE - LATER

Angel is watching, Cordy still on his shoulder. (A little drool, but no way he's changing position.)

ANGLE: THE PRIMA BALLERINA

We are close on her as she dances.

Angel watches, the quiet excitement gradually giving way to something else. Something nagging at him.

ANGLE: WESLEY

Still glances at Fred. She looks back once, smiles. Wesley turns his attention back to the ballet and we push in on him, slowly, until:

11 INT. STAGE - NIGHT

We see the action on stage -- only now it is FRED dancing, alone. She is every inch the delicate ballerina, dancing a graceful, lonely solo.

After a minute or so, WESLEY runs on stage, also in full ballet regalia. To say he looks silly is to truth-tell. He prances about like a special-needs gazelle, courting the fair Fred, who is initially hesitant. But then he comes up to her and he's suddenly a lot less silly in close up. She turns slowly into his arms, the two of them about to kiss --

12 INT. AUDITORIUM/STAGE - LATER

Wild applause brings Wesley out of his reverie. The curtain is closing on act one. Gunn is whistling, clapping -- if he had a big foam rubber "number one" hand, by God he'd be using it.

Cordy wakes with a start --

CORDELIA
I loved it!

ANGEL
It's just intermission.

He's clearly still puzzling something out. Cordy looks at his jacket.

CORDELIA
That isn't drool, is it?

ANGEL
It's okay. Matches the back.

Everyone is getting up for intermission. Our gang follows suit.

13 INT. LOBBY OF THEATRE - NIGHT

Our gang is keeping away from the biggest crush of the crowd.

> GUNN
> I'll say it once and gloat all you want: These guys
> are tight, and I am tripping out.

> WESLEY
> They certainly live up to their reputation. Has the
> choreography changed much since --

> ANGEL
> No. Nothing's changed.

> WESLEY
> Well, it's wonderful that they're able to --

> ANGEL
> No. I mean nothing's changed. These are the same
> dancers I saw before.

> FRED
> That's impossible! We're watching the exact same
> troupe you saw in 1990?

> GUNN
> Un, I think he said 1890.

> FRED
> Oh. Okay, that's much more impossible.

> ANGEL
> So, somebody wanna tell me how we're watching a show
> starring people who should have died sixty years ago?

There's a beat, as they all think.

> CORDELIA
> Well, it's a puzzler. Are there snacks?

BLACK OUT.

<u>END OF ACT ONE</u>

<u>ACT TWO</u>

14 INT. LOBBY OF THEATRE - MOMENTS LATER

They are discussing possibilities.

> WESLEY
> So what are we thinking? Vampires?

> CORDELIA
> They're not a deeply tanned bunch...

> GUNN
> That would also explain the precision, and the
> athleticism. I mean, some of those jumps...
> (off their looks)
> You know, I was cool before I met y'all.

> CORDELIA
> Dancing vampires. Who's not scared?

159

                        ANGEL
         (shaking his head)
     Not it. I'd know. I'd sense it.

                        WESLEY
     Even all the way back there?
         (oops)
     With the... panoramic view...

                        FRED
     Zombies! Or would they be peeling...?

                        WESLEY
     Some kind of spell.

                        ANGEL
     Possibly. I figure we better check it out.

                        FRED
     Maybe after the show we can head backstage --

                        ANGEL
     I was thinking now.

                        GUNN
     Okay, but there might be a clue, you know, IN the
     performance, maybe some of us should... watch...

                        WESLEY
         (to Angel)
     You created him, only you can destroy him.

Gunn hits the grinning Wes on the arm.

                        ANGEL
     You guys go back. I'll snoop.

                        CORDELIA
     I'm with snoopy. Magic of the ballet not really
     getting to me.

                        WESLEY
     How will the dancers keep time without your rhythmic
     snoring?

                        GUNN
     Oh, that's too cold.

The lights flicker -- time to go back.

                        CORDELIA
         (to Wes)
     Don't think that's not coming back to haunt you.

                        ANGEL
     Go.

The trio moves back to their seats. Angel and Cordy heading in the other
direction.

                        CORDELIA
     I didn't really snore, did I?

ANGEL
Of course not.

15 INT. OUTSIDE THE BACKSTAGE ENTRANCE - MOMENTS LATER

ANGLE ON: A big fat cornfed giant of a SECURITY GUARD, standing in front of a
door marked: BACKSTAGE. ABSOLUTELY NO ADMITTANCE.

REVERSE ON Cordy and Angel, checking him out at a distance.

                    CORDELIA
          Check out the zeppelin.

                    ANGEL
          Awful lotta muscle for a ballet company.

                    CORDELIA
          You want I should distract him?
          (seductive)
          Make with the nice nice while you slip by?

                    ANGEL
          Don't be stupid.

She is stung, but before she can reply --

                    ANGEL (cont'd)
          I'm THAT guy, and the most beautiful woman I've ever
          seen is making eyes at me? That's either a bachelor
          party, or a scam.

                    CORDELIA
          What did you just call me?

                    ANGEL
          I'm sorry. You're not stupid.

                    CORDELIA
          No, after that.

                    ANGEL
          (all business)
          I think I'm gonna have to go with my patented Sudden
          Burst of Violence.

                    CORDELIA
          Eh, hold on. I may have an approach that's a little
          more subtle.

SMASH CUT TO:

16 INT. SAME - MOMENTS LATER

Cordelia stands in front of the security guard.

                    CORDELIA
          Say, do you like bribes?

                    SECURITY GUARD (beaming)
          Do I ever!

Cordelia casually holds up a $20.

>   CORDELIA
>   We really wanna go backstage.

>   SECURITY GUARD
>   Okay, see, but that's not so much a bribe as it is a
>   tip. And since I'm not parking your car, there's no
>   way --

WHAM! Angel decks him across the chin.

The guy takes the hit and then just turns back and glares at Angel.

>   CORDELIA
>   (counting out more $20s)
>   Oookay...

>   ANGEL
>   (to the guard)
>   And that's just a taste of... you see I really wasn't
>   warmed up.

>   SECURITY GUARD
>   I used to fight pro. And I'd say you're... about to
>   find out... what...

He drops.

>   ANGEL
>   OKAY! That's how we do it.

They open the door, head into

17 INT. BACKSTAGE - CONTINUING
We see the door as Cordelia and Angel step inside -- it's clearly old here,
though everything beyond the door is modern. They shut it, looking ahead with a
certain degree of wonder.

>   CORDELIA
>   Okay. You saw the building when we drove by -- do you
>   remember it going on forever?

ANGLE: Over them down the hallway. In fact, it does go on forever, with many
hallways branching off. In addition to being an endless maze, it's very clearly
the backstage of a turn-of-the-century theatre, all dark wood and gas lamps, old
flyers and random props and scenery scattered about.

>   ANGEL
>   This is clearly a spell, or a time flux or something.
>   I don't think we wanna be rushing in here.

>   CORDELIA
>   Let's get the others, talk options.

Angel is looking back the way they came.

>   ANGEL
>   Yeah...

ANGLE: THE DOOR is gone, and the hallway extends forever in THAT direction as
well.

Works in theory...

18 INT. AUDITORIUM/STAGE - CONTINUING

The dance continues.

Our trio watches, Fred in the middle.

19 INT. BACKSTAGE HALL OUTSIDE DRESSING ROOM - LATER

Cordy and Angel turn a corner.

> ANGEL
> Okay, there has to be something here besides this
> maze.

> CORDELIA
> And with our luck it'll be a Minotaur or a giant Ms.
> Pac Man.

> ANGEL
> Do you hear that?

There is a faint sound. A sobbing, wheezing sound.

> CORDELIA
> Someone laughing.

> ANGEL
> Or crying?

> CORDELIA
> Or both... Okay, officially creeped...

> ANGEL
> Look.

He indicates a door. It's ajar. They move slowly toward it. He opens it and they enter.

20 INT. DRESSING ROOM - CONTINUING

They enter, slowly, looking around. It is opulent clutter -- clearly the dressing room of a turn of the century diva. There is a standing screen for changing, a plush red divan, plus the make-up station, brushes and paints laid out.

Cordy and Angel move silently around the room, examining things, touching them -- the energy of the place is very mellow and surreal, and their energy matches it. The room touches them.

They speak quietly.

> ANGEL
> This is her dressing room.

> CORDELIA
> The Prima Ballerina.

> ANGEL
> It's unchanged.

He runs his hand along the back of the divan. Cordelia sits at the mirror, picks up the hairbrush.

                    CORDELIA
          She would wait for him here...

                    ANGEL
          What?

Not answering, Cordelia puts the brush back and looks in the mirror. Unformed questions and half-answers playing through her mind. She picks up a long neck-lace with a tiny cross attached, bejewelled and elegant.

                    ANGEL (cont'd)
          It's warm... it's very warm.

She stands and they are close, looking around. There is a slight sheen of sweat on their faces.

                    CORDELIA
          I feel it.

                    ANGEL
          Something happened here.

                    CORDELIA
          Angel.

                    ANGEL
          Yes.

                    CORDELIA
          I want you to undress me.

                    ANGEL
          (struggling)
          You what?

                    CORDELIA
          It's just another costume. I want you to see who I
          really am. You're the only one who can.

                    ANGEL
          I...
          (fighting it)
          This isn't us. Cordelia, we're... acting this out.
          Someone is --

                    CORDELIA
          (coming out of it)
          Whoah.

                    ANGEL
          The energy in this room, it's...

                    CORDELIA
          Did I actually just tell you to undress me?

He falls right back into it, getting closer to her.

                    ANGEL
          Is that what you want?

                    CORDELIA
          (slipping)
          Please, I --

                    ANGEL
          You want me to make love to you right here?

                    CORDELIA
          You know I do.

Their hands have begun roaming, touching hair, shoulders, backs... their faces
inches apart.

                    ANGEL
          But you're afraid.

                    CORDELIA
          What if he finds us?

                    ANGEL
          I'm not afraid. I'm not afraid of anything.

He pulls her close. They're gonna kiss. Her lips so close to his...

                    CORDELIA
          (whispers)
          I'm only alive... when you're inside me...

And kiss they do. Big time.

                    END OF ACT TWO

                    ACT THREE

21 INT. DRESSING ROOM

Well, they're still kissing. It's pretty heated, I must say.

Cordelia brings her hand to his cheek -- the hand with the little cross dan-
gling. It swings against his cheek and he pulls away briefly, regaining some of
his composure, as does she.

                    ANGEL
          Cordelia...

                    CORDELIA
          Yes...

                    ANGEL
          I'm sorry.

                    CORDELIA
          No... We need to be out of here.

                    ANGEL
          Yes.

They move close again, about to kiss --

                    CORDELIA
This isn't out of here.

                    ANGEL
No. Right.

They force themselves to the door, always managing to keep in close contact. When they reach it, he is behind her and he moves his arm around her to get the door, she arches back into him, one arm up to cup the back of his head. . .

                    CORDELIA
      (pure lust)
Open the damn door...

                    ANGEL
Kinda hard...

                    CORDELIA
Kinda noticed...

He does open it, and they slip out into --

22 INT. BACKSTAGE HALL OUTSIDE DRESSING ROOM

They come out actually catching their breath. Shut the door behind them.

                    CORDELIA
Whoah.

                    ANGEL
That's a fair assessment.

                    CORDELIA
What the hell is that place?

                    ANGEL
There's spirits in there. Energy, trapped in time...
took us over.

                    CORDELIA
Yee scary. Good thing it wears off right away.

Wide on Angel as he takes off his jacket and casually holds it in front of his pants.

                    ANGEL
Yeah. Good thing.

23 INT. ANGEL'S HOTEL - ANGEL'S BEDROOM - NIGHT

We see Connor being laid into the crib, all sleepy, by two green hands.

Lorne lays him down, singing softly the classic lullaby:

                    LORNE
Go to sleep/ lullaby/ you've been fed and you're
sleepy/ you'll be with/ Uncle Lorne/ who in no way
resents not being asked to go to the ballet/ and is
certainly/ not thinking/ of selling you to the first
vampire cult that makes him a decent offer...

24 INT. ANGEL'S HOTEL - LOBBY

We are in the Steadicam POV of an unknown presence as it enters the lobby, looking around and heading up the stairs. (The score should continue in lullaby mode, but, needless to say, creepy.)

25 INT. ANGEL'S HOTEL - ANGEL'S BEDROOM - MOMENTS LATER

Lorne turns, senses alerted.

>   LORNE
>   You just sleep on, little nipper, Uncle Lorne's gonna
>   make sure we're alone.

He quietly crosses the room, picking up a battle axe on the way. Looks back at the crib.

>   LORNE (cont'd)
>   Won't be gone a moment...

As he is speaking, the door is opening behind him. He turns --

We REVERSE over the dark figure that enters, as Host takes step back, eyes wide.

>   LORNE (cont'd)
>   Oh, my God.

26 INT. BACKSTAGE HALL OUTSIDE DRESSING ROOM - CONTIUING

Angel and Cordy are starting down the hall.

>   CORDELIA
>   You sure this is the way?

>   ANGEL
>   I'm sure it's "a" way... Place is a maze, I'm just
>   hoping we'll find another room that --

>   CORDELIA
>   Dammit.

She has stopped. He turns to her.

>   ANGEL
>   What?

>   CORDELIA
>   I said something. Back in that room, something
>   important. Do you remember?

>   ANGEL
>   (uncomfy)
>   Uh... you're only alive when I'm --

>   CORDELIA
>   Not that.

>   ANGEL
>   No. Of course. I was just... Oh! Hey! I said you were
>   afraid.

                    CORDELIA
    And I said "what if he finds us."

                    ANGEL
    She had a secret lover.

                    CORDELIA
    They were afraid of someone. And I'll bet you anything
    that someone is the reason we're stuck here.
    (frustrated)
    We left too soon.

                    ANGEL
    We -- who? The room?

                    CORDELIA
    It's a clue! Those spirits, or energy or whatever, are
    still in there so we can find out what happened! We
    have to go back in.

                    ANGEL
    I'm marvelling at the wrongness of that idea.

                    CORDELIA
    You wanna wander around backstage like Spinal Tap for
    the next... ever?

                    ANGEL
    I'm sure there's other rooms that --

                    CORDELIA
    All we have to do is play the scene out. Say what they
    have to say, and get out before... before I give you a
    happy.

                    ANGEL
    What if there is no more talking in that scene? Look,
    I've been possessed by the spirits of old lovers
    before, it never goes well.

                    CORDELIA
    I've got my little cross, if things get out of hand...
    Hey, it's awkward, but it's not us, so as long as
    nothing is removed or inserted, it's all forgotten.

                    ANGEL
    It is us, Cordelia. You and me. And kissing you,
    it's...

He's close to a confession here...

                    ANGEL (cont'd)
    It's not something I can just --

                    CORDELIA
    Oh, come on. It's not that horrible.

She turns to go back, totally missing his point.

                    CORDELIA (cont'd)
    Up to his ass in demon gore, fine, but ask him to
    mack on a hottie and he wigs. My champion, ladies
    and gentlemen.

27 INT. AUDITORIUM/STAGE - NIGHT

The dance continues. Gunn, Fred and Wesley all watch intently.

ANGLE: WESLEY'S HAND

Is inching toward Fred's, about to slide over it, Wesley completely unaware that --

ANGLE: GUNN'S HAND

Is doing the exact same thing on the opposite side.

It's a turtle race as both boys try to make the subtle move, Fred aware of neither. And the winner is:

>   FRED
>   Angel!

Hands withdraw.

>   GUNN
>   Huh?

>   WESLEY
>   What?

>   FRED
>   And Cordy! They've been gone way too long.

>   WESLEY
>   You're right. Come on.

They start shuffling out.

>   GUNN
>   But... we're gonna miss the end...

28 INT. DRESSING ROOM - CONTINUING

Angel and Cordy are in, they're looking about themselves uncomfortably...

>   ANGEL
>   Anything coming?

>   CORDELIA
>   Uhhh... okay.
>   (claps her hands, motivation time)
>   Let's take it from the middle.
>   (moves into position)
>   I want you... undress me.

She is completely uninspired and wooden, rushing through it, and he is as well.

>   ANGEL
>   You want me to have sex now with you here?

>   CORDELIA
>   Yes! But I'm scared.

>   ANGEL
>   But you're afraid.

> CORDELIA
> And I'm afraid. What if we, he finds us?!

> ANGEL
> He who?
> (off her look)
> Urn, but I'm not afraid of anything.

He takes her stiffly in his arms.

> CORDELIA (mumbles)
> Only good inside blah blah blah --

KISS! Which is a microsmack, both mouths closed, not exactly act break material. Both wait for a moment -- anything?

> ANGEL (looking around)
> Maybe it only works the one time, if the energy is --

Cordy kisses the living shit out of him.

29 INT. OUTSIDE THE BACKSTAGE ENTRANCE - CONTINUING

Wesley, Fred and Gunn approach the doorway. The security guard is still out cold. As they step over him...

> GUNN
> At least Angel left us a trail...

ANGLE: OVER TWO FIGURES IN BLACK to the group, a distance away. A moment, and the figures take off.

30 INT. BOX SEAT, THEATRE - MOMENTS LATER

The Count is watching the show. The figures appear by him again, we see nothing much of them but black. There is whispering, and the Count's face darkens.

> THE COUNT
> Deal with them. I can't be bothered right now.

ANGLE: The Count's POV of the stage: as the dance continues.

31 INT. DRESSING ROOM - LATER

Cordy comes swiftly down onto the divan. Angel on top of her. His tie is undone, his shirt open. They are kissing, hands everywhere. He lowers himself, kissing her neck, her collarbone...

> CORDELIA
> This is wrong...

> ANGEL
> Hush...

> CORDELIA
> You don't know him. He has power.

Angel looks her right in the eye.

> ANGEL
> The power to do this?

We don't see exactly what he's referring to, but she breathes in sharply, eyes squeezing shut for an instant. But there is still fear in them as she breathlessly continues...

                    CORDELIA
          I'm not... Stefan, his power is unnatural. He could --

                    ANGEL
          What. Kill us?

                    CORDELIA
          Worse.

                    ANGEL
          Kurskov owns the company. He doesn't own you.

                    CORDELIA
          He doesn't know that.
                (bitterly)
          He thinks I'm his. That I dance for him. He's nothing
          but a deluded fan... He thinks I love him.

                    ANGEL
          Come away with me. Now. Tonight. We'll disappear. Even
          HE won't find us.

                    CORDELIA
          I... Stefan, everything I've worked for is here...

                    ANGEL
          You can still dance.

                    CORDELIA
          Can I? I don't... Not yet. Maybe when we're...

                    ANGEL
                (terse)
          Don't. Don't make promises.

She takes his head, brings it to her bosom, overcome, near tears.

                    CORDELIA
          Help me... help me be not afraid...

32 INT. BACKSTAGE CORRIDOR - CONTINUING

Wes, Fred and Gunn are making their cautious way down a corridor.

                    GUNN
          This is very not right.

                    FRED
          Do you hear --

A shadow moves across them -- they look, but no one is there.

                    WESLEY
          There's something...

Faintly, they can hear a woman moaning and crying out.

> WESLEY (cont'd)
> Someone's in pain.

Fred listens harder. A rising, breathy moan.

> FRED
> Either that, or someone's in fun.

33 INT. DRESSING ROOM - CONTINUING

We're tight on Cordy as Angel slips the straps of her dress
over her shoulders --

-- tight on her stomach as the dress is slipped down. Angel
kissing her bare belly --

-- tight on her face, struggling, succumbing --

> CORDELIA
> No... oh, no...

She looks over at the doorway --

> CORDELIA (cont'd)
> Oh, no!

CLOSE ON ANGEL as he sits up, looking as well, and is TACKLED over the back of
the divan by a FIGURE in black.

They go flying into a heap in the corner, the figure punching Angel hard while
he's on the ground.

ANGLE: From behind the divan, we see Cordy pop up, no visible dress but the back
of the divan hiding anything truly relevant. She's harried -- herself again.
Watches the figure hit Angel --

> CORDELIA (cont'd)
> Oh, thank god.

Angel snaps back from a blow, grabs the guy on top of him and pushes him back,
getting his first good look at him: His face is that of a comedy mask, forever
grinning. Angel takes a moment to register the creepiness, then hits the guy so
hard he goes flying onto his back, off of Angel.

Cordy is pulling up her straps, dressed again --

> CORDELIA (cont'd)
> Okay, good; so they were probably interrupted by this
> Count Kurskov or his lackeys, right? So we're done
> with the --

As she's saying this, the OTHER FIGURE in black, with the face of pure tragedy,
is emerging behind her.

Angel runs toward her --

> CORDELIA (cont'd)
> (ducking)
> We're done!

-- and leaps over the couch, tackling Tragedy.

Cordy looks around at the new action -- as Comedy rises behind her and pulls a sword and dagger.

34 INT. LARGE BACKSTAGE SPACE - CONTINUING

Fred, Wes and Gunn hear nearby crashing --

                    GUNN
          Now that sounds less like fun --

And an identical Tragedy comes up and STABS him in the back

                    GUNN (cont'd)
          Gahh!

                    FRED
          Charles!

BLACK OUT.

                    END OF ACT THREE

                    ACT FOUR

35 INT. LARGE BACKSTAGE SPACE

Gunn slams his elbow into Tragedy's face, sending him back as Wes spins to see Comedy coming from the other side, both blades drawn.

                    WESLEY
          Fred, stay between us.

                              GUNN
                    I need to...

He drops, grimacing. Fred rushes to him -- sees Tragedy coming, grabs a prop and
swings it mightily into his face, knocking him back. His sword and dagger fly
free and she grabs the sword --

                              FRED
                    Wesley!

And throws it to Wes, who catches it handily and begins fencing with Comedy,
driving him back. He calls out to Fred:

                              WESLEY
                    Can you handle the other?

Looks back briefly to see Fred beating the guy to a pulp with her big prop.
Turns back to Comedy.

                              WESLEY (cont'd)
                    Well then. Just us.

And he continues driving him back, into the hall nearby.

36 INT. DRESSING ROOM - CONTINUING

Cordy is trying to get away from Comedy, knocking the screen over onto him,
casting about for a weapon --

                              CORDELIA
                    Little help...

ANGLE: ANGEL as he has Tragedy on the ground, is forcing down his sword hand --
Tragedy stabs him in the chest --

                              ANGEL
                    Thank you --

He rears back, knife in chest, both hands now free to grab the sword, flip it
into his hand, pull the knife free and while stabbing Tragedy in the heart
throwing the knife without even looking --

-- whip pan -- THWUNK!

Right into the throat of Comedy.

Cordy comes to Angel.

                              ANGEL (cont'd)
                    You all right?

                              CORDELIA
                    Yeah. We gotta move.

                              ANGEL
                    You think they're not dead?

                              CORDELIA
                    You just looked really hot doing that.

                              ANGEL
                    (getting it)
                    Oh.

     CORDELIA
  Yeah.

     ANGEL
  Run.

They head for the door.

37 INT. BACKSTAGE CORRIDOR - CONTINUING

Wesley still drives Comedy back in fierce battle.

38 INT. LARGE BACKSTAGE SPACE - CONTINUING

Gunn YELLS in pain as Fred pulls at his shirt, looking at his wound. She is
pale and frantic. It's kinda bloody.

     FRED
  Oh god Oh god --

     GUNN
  It's not -- OW! It's not that deep. It didn't go that
  deep.

FRED
Charles, there's blood...

GUNN
There usually is. I been cut worse than this. I just
need to wrap it --

FRED
Of course --

She grabs a piece of fabric, RIPS off a piece --

39 INT. BACKSTAGE CORRIDOR - CONTINUING

Wesley finally knocks aside the dagger and rapier and DRIVES his sword home
through Comedy's chest, coming up right in his face.

WESLEY
Who's laughing now?

Comedy continues to giggle as he fades...

WESLEY (cont'd)
Well, you, but I still win.

Wesley yanks his sword free and Comedy drops.

40 INT. LARGE BACKSTAGE SPACE - CONTINUING

Fred has tied the fabric around Gunn's waist.

GUNN
That's good. Should hold.

He sees how flustered and pale she is.

GUNN (cont'd)
You okay? You hurt?

FRED
I'm fine, I just thought -- I'm sorry, I shouldn't
fall apart like this...

GUNN
(smiles)
Scared I'm gonna die on you?

FRED
Charles, don't even --

GUNN
All I ask is... one last kiss... as the light is dim-
ming...

FRED
(upset)
You think that's funny?

GUNN
It's just a scratch!

FRED
But I thought it was... I...

She's near tears. He stops joking. Understands the depth of
her feeling.

                    GUNN
          Hey. Heyyy...

They are close enough for him to put his hands on her arms. He reaches up to
her hair, strokes it. They speak more softly, their faces close.

                    GUNN (cont'd)
          You really that worried about me?

                    FRED
          Probably think I'm an idiot.

                    GUNN
          I think if you care that much... the wound is defi-
          nitely deep.

                    FRED (smiles softly)
          The light is dimming?

                    GUNN
          And all I ask... is one... last...

Kiss. Long, soft, sweet as spun sugar.

We see the two of them, in tableau, alone in the room, kissing each other for
the first time. PULL BACK to reveal, at right of frame, the body of Wesley as
he silently has arrived on scene. At left of frame there is a smooth surface of
some kind, a prop door or something, in which we see Wesley's face reflected.

His face. The weight on him.

He silently backs out of the room.

41 INT. BACKSTAGE CORRIDOR - CONTINUING

Wesley walks a few steps away -- and drops to his knees. Looks up, sudden rage
filling his expression.

ANGLE: COMEDY

As his eyes pop back open.

42 INT. STAGE - CONTINUING

The dance.

43 INT. LARGE BACKSTAGE SPACE - LATER

Angel and Cordy rush in -- from a different entrance. Fred is helping Gunn up.
They are both a little giddy, though still serious.

                    ANGEL
          You guys all right?

                    FRED
          Charles got stabbed.

                    GUNN
          Couple stitches worth.

                    ANGEL
          (sees Tragedy)
          Same guys that attacked us.

                    FRED
          Uh, Cordy? Your, uh, tag is showing.

ANGLE: THE PRICE TAG sticks out the back of Cordy's dress. Fred slips it in.

                    GUNN
          Any idea where we are, or what the Hell?

                    ANGEL
          Yeah. Cordy and I hit a kind of mystical hot spot. In
          one of the dressing rooms.

                    CORDELIA
          Seems like the Prima Ballerina had a lover back in
          the day, and there was a Count Kurskov who owned the
          company. I guess he had a thing for the girl, and
          they were mightily afraid of him.

                    ANGEL
          He had power of some kind...

                    WESLEY
          He's a Wizard.

He enters, betraying nothing of his pain but totally serious.

                    WESLEY (cont'd)
          He was obsessed with the girl. When he found her
          with the other man, he went insane with jealous rage.
          Pulled her out of time, out of any reality beyond his
          theatre, his company. He swore she would dance for
          him forever.

                    FRED
          How did you --

                    WESLEY
          I hit a hot spot, too.

                    GUNN
          And now we're stuck here?

                    WESLEY
          Well... this kind of temporal shift can't just exist,
          it has to be maintained. Takes power and concentration.
          If we can overload him somehow, we might be able to
          slip back to the real world.

                    GUNN
          Man with a plan.

Wesley stares at Gunn a moment, says nothing.

                    ANGEL
          Great. So how do we overload him?

                    WESLEY
          Well, I imagine that requires some energy...

He indicates the side of the room, where Tragedy has risen again and is shaking, splitting... and becoming two Tragedys.

Before they can get their bearings. Angel steps up and grabs them both in separate headlocks, jerking his arms up and snapping their necks. They drop to the ground -- and begin to shake as they did before.

Wesley looks down the corridor:

ANGLE: DOWN THE CORRIDOR come two Comedies.

> FRED
> The more we kill, the more he makes.

> CORDELIA
> Look!

ANGLE: A WALL which is old, briefly shimmers and becomes modern. Then back.

> WESLEY
> And that's draining his energy. Angel, you try to find a way towards the stage. The Count will be watching.

> ANGEL
> I bet he has a box...

> WESLEY
> Find his power source and destroy it. We'll do our best to loosen his hold.

> GUNN
> By making more monsters. Man with a frightening plan.

> WESLEY
> Angel, go.

More are approaching. The gang weapons up while Angel takes off, pausing to roundhouse a Comedy in the face.

> CORDELIA
> Back here. They can't surround us.

The group heads for a corner slightly boxed in with scenery. Wesley turns to Fred and Gunn.

> WESLEY
> You two.
> (a beat)
> Stay close together.

He turns back to the approaching group, now five strong.

> WESLEY (cont'd)
> I'll take point.

> CORDELIA
> Hope you're in a killin' mood.

> WESLEY
> I should do all right.

And he knocks a sword side and STABS --

44 INT. BACKSTAGE CORRIDOR - CONTINUING

Angel comes around a corner, looks back -- not sure where he is.

45 INT. LARGE BACKSTAGE SPACE -
A Comedy goes flying against a wall, head cracking.

46 INT. BACKSTAGE CORRIDOR - CONTINUING

Angel sees a wall shimmer -- beyond it is the stage, seen from behind. Without hesitating he dives through the 'hole', which closes back up right after.

47 INT. WINGS/STAGE - CONTINUING

Angel is in the corner. He sees:

ANGLE: THE PERFORMERS on stage, still dancing. Some of them leap off stage and as they do they simply disappear, reappearing as they re-enter the scene.

Angel's eye is drawn to the front of the wings, where there is one person standing quietly. It is the Prima Ballerina, waiting for her cue.

> ANGEL
> Hello...

> THE DANCER
> (startled)
> Who are you? There's no one... you're new.

> ANGEL
> I'm pretty old, actually. I've seen you dance.

As they speak, she barely turns to him, always keeping ready to go back on.

> THE DANCER
> Everyone sees me.

> ANGEL
> It was Giselle then as well.

> THE DANCER
> Always.

> ANGEL
> I know what's happening. Count Kurskov, he's punishing you.

He follows her look to see:

ANGLE: THE COUNT in his box on the other side of the stage.

> THE DANCER
> He made me. He owns me. When I dance, it's only for him.

> ANGEL
> Do you believe that?

> THE DANCER
> It really doesn't matter. I'll dance, I'll wait here, then I'll dance again. That's all.

                    ANGEL
          A hundred years, doing the same piece every night...
          is that enough? What about Stefan?

The name affects her.

                    THE DANCER
          I waited too long. I should have gone when he asked
          me, should have disappeared. But I wanted this, this
          dance, this... I hesitated and I lost everything that
          mattered. Now all I do is wait.

                    ANGEL
          You dance...

She takes a moment before explaining:

                    THE DANCER
          There's a section in the first act, during the
          courtship dance, where my foot slips. My ankle is
          turned, and I don't quite hold... every time. He
          doesn't notice. He doesn't even know ballet that well.
          But always, at that same moment, I slip.

Finally she turns to him.

                    THE DANCER (cont'd)
          It isn't just the same ballet. It's the same
          performance. I don't dance. I echo.

She turns back to the stage.

                    THE DANCER (cont'd)
          Please... can you make it stop?

48 INT. LARGE BACKSTAGE SPACE - CONTINUING

A quick shot of our gang BESIEGED by Comedies and Tragedies, fighting heroically.

                    WESLEY
          It's working!

                    GUNN
          Yeah, there's dozens of 'em. Yay us.

                    WESLEY
          It's gotta be weakening his hold.

49 INT. WINGS/STAGE - CONTINUING

Angel puts his hand out on stage but it disappears. He pulls it back. Looks up
at The Count, at the Dancer.

                    ANGEL
          I can help you. But you have to do something.

                    THE DANCER
          What?

                    ANGEL
          You have to change the ending. Dance something new.

                         THE DANCER
                  I can't...

Angel sees:

ANGLE: A WALL of ropes and old fashioned levers becomes a modern wall with
electric equipment. Then back.

                              ANGEL
                  He doesn't control all this. He's losing it. But you
                  have to take the stage.

He comes closer to her.

                              ANGEL (cont'd)
                  It's not too late. You can change things.

She looks at him in fear -- then rushes on stage.

She dances toward a waiting gentleman -- then stops, changes the choreography,
moves away. The man simply fades into nothingness.

ANGLE: IN THE BOX The Count rises, freaking.

ON STAGE, the Dancer does the same thing, making another phantom dancer fade
away.

Angel sticks his hand on stage. It doesn't disappear.

50 INT. LARGE BACKSTAGE SPACE - CONTINUING

As Wesley viciously kills yet another Comedy --

51 INT. BOX SEAT, THEATRE - CONTINUING

As The Count is sweating, too much to control... ANGLE: ON STAGE runs Angel,
crossing and LEAPING into the box.

                              ANGEL
                  Hey, where's your power center?

                              THE COUNT
                  How dare you --

                              ANGEL
                  I'll guess.

He punches The Count right in his bejewelled medal, shattering the stone and
staggering The Count as a flash of light bursts momentarily from the broken
jewel.

Angel looks on stage, where the Dancer is alone. She looks at him gratefully,
then lays herself out in a graceful bow, fading as she does.

52 INT. ACTUAL MODERN BACKSTAGE - CONTINUING

ANGLE: The audience. Confusedly, they slowly begin to applaud.

Our gang finds themselves alone. A beat, as they look around...

53 INT. BOX SEAT, THEATRE - CONTINUING

The Count is nearly having a heart attack, clutching his chest.

> THE COUNT
> You've no right...

> ANGEL
> Save it.

> THE COUNT
> She was... she was my love... she danced... for me...

> ANGEL
> Yeah. You love her that much?

HE PUNCHES him again, sending sprawling into his seat, where he labors for breath...

> ANGEL (cont'd)
> Start a website.

Angel walks disgustedly away.

54 INT. ANGEL'S HOTEL - OFFICE - NIGHT

The gang has returned. Wes is sewing up Gunn, who is being as manly as possible. Fred is helping.

> WESLEY
> You should clean it. Do you need anything for the pain?

> GUNN (looking at Fred)
> What pain?

They share a smile that Wesley does not comment on. Gunn heads to the bathroom.

55 INT. ANGEL'S HOTEL- LOBBY - CONTINUING

Angel and Cordy are trying not to be awkward with each other. Cordy is examining her dress.

> CORDELIA
> You think I can still return it? 'cause otherwise we're gonna have to take a lot more cases.

> ANGEL
> Cordy, urn...

> CORDELIA
> You know, we should probably just not talk about our little adventure. Anything that might have been seen, anything that might have been, oh, perky --

> ANGEL
> I just wanna pretend it never happened.

> CORDELIA
> Exactly.

> ANGEL
> Wipe it from my memory.

                    CORDELIA
               (complete reversal)
          Well, what, was it like disgusting?

                    ANGEL
          No, I... I would just want, if we were to... I'd want
          it to be, urn, new. Start at the beginning.

                    CORDELIA
          Lost me in the middle.

                    ANGEL
          Cordy, we've been working together a long time, and...
          I mean you've become... a truly extraordinary woman. I
          know we haven't always gotten along, but I really
          think we... you know we...

A radiant smile sweeps onto her face.

                    CORDELIA
          Groo...

                    ANGEL
          Yes, we grew, un, closer together, and I was --

She is moving toward him, past him, he turns to see her pick up speed and throw
herself into the arms of...

                    CORDELIA
          GROO!

It is in fact the GROOSALUGG, the Brave and Undefeated. Fred and Wes emerge as
he sweeps Cordy up, spinning her and setting her back down, joy on his face.

                    GROOSALUGG
          Princess.

                    CORDELIA
          Oh, my God. I can't believe it's you.

                    GROOSALUGG
          I feared you'd forget who I was.

                    CORDELIA
          Remind me.

And they kiss.

Angel watches. Host coming next to him. Lorne is well aware of Angel's feelings.

                    LORNE
          Just showed up. Apparently, once everyone on Pylea got
          their freedom, political situation got kind of
          sketchy. The Groosalugg here got deposed -- they set
          up some kind of people's republic.
               (weakly)
          So he came looking for his... true love...

                    ANGEL
          Well, that's... that's good for her.

                    LORNE
          Yeah.

                    ANGEL
          I think I'll check on Connor.

                    LORNE
          He's sleeping --

But Angel has already left.

ANGLE: FRED AND WES

As they watch Cordy and Groo whisper to each other. Fred looks pleased for her
but concerned.

                    FRED
          Well, that's a surprise. I thought for sure she was
          meant to be with Angel. I guess you can never predict
          those things.
          (turning back)
          You know?

Wesley looks at her.

56 INT. STAGE - NIGHT

And we see, briefly, Fred dancing, twirling around, graceful, beautiful.

57 INT. ANGEL'S HOTEL - LOBBY - CONTINUING

                    WESLEY
          No. I guess you never can.

He smiles politely. Looks away. Looks back. We hold on him.

BLACK OUT

                         THE END

ANGEL
"Waiting in the Wings"

SET LIST INTERIORS

ANGEL'S HOTEL
      LOBBY/GARDEN
      ANGEL'S BEDROOM
      LOBBY
      OFFICE

THEATRE
      BOX SEAT
      AUDITORIUM/STAGE
      STAGE
      LOBBY OF THEATRE
      OUTSIDE THE BACKSTAGE ENTRANCE
      BACKSTAGE
      BACKSTAGE HALL OUTSIDE DRESSING ROOM
      DRESSING ROOM
      BACKSTAGE CORRIDOR
      LARGE BACKSTAGE SPACE
      WINGS/STAGE
      ACTUAL MODERN BACKSTAGE

FANCY CLOTHING STORE

SET LIST EXTERIORS

THEATRE - NIGHT

ANGEL™

issue five   scriptbook

Episode
Five by Five

Written By
JIM KOUF

ANGEL™
"FIVE BY FIVE"

WRITTEN BY

JIM KOUF

Starring:
DAVID BOREANAZ
CHARISMA CARPENTER
ALEXIS DENISOF
ELIZA DUSHKU
JULIE BENZ
CHRISTIAN KANE
THOMAS BURR
STEPHANIE ROMANOV
RAINBOW BORDEN
FRANCIS FALLON
ADRIENNE JANICK
RODRICK FOX
THOR EDGELL
JENNIFER SLIMKO
TYLER CHRISTOPHER

Created By
JOSS WHEDON & DAVID GREENWALT

Written By
JIM KOUF

<u>TEASER</u>

1 EXT. DOWNTOWN - NIGHT

Near the Los Angeles concrete river and railroad tracks. Rusting chain link
fences, old bridges with eerie yellow fluorescent lighting, brick buildings
covered with graffiti.

A MAN walks past the graffiti covered wall. His head is shaved. He's about
twenty-five. Wears a flannel shirt, baggy pants. He's not afraid in this
part of town. It's his territory. Under the flannel shirt, a tank top. We
see lots of tattoo work on his neck, maybe a little creeping out onto his
wrists and a teardrop beneath one eye. HE'S A GANG BANGER.

We FOLLOW Gang Banger as he crosses the street, heading for a bridge. IN THE
DISTANCE, we can SEE FLAMES rising from a FIVE GALLON DRUM. And the FIGURES
OF THREE MEN standing around it.

2 EXT. UNDER THE BRIDGE - NIGHT

One of the Gang's hangouts. A BURNED OUT HULK OF A CAR. A couple old
couches and chairs. Lots of graffiti.

GANG BANGER ENTERS THE DOMAIN, MOVES TOWARD THE THREE FIGURES GATHERED
AROUND THE FIRE IN THE FIVE GALLON DRUM. Their backs are to us so we can't
see their faces yet. They look like bangers from here.

                    GANG BANGER
          Ese, what the hell're you burnin' in there? It
          stinks like --

Gang Banger stops, realizing these guys aren't his pals.

                    GANG BANGER (cont'd)
          Hey, you hangin' in the wrong place. My boys ain't
          gonna be too happy when they get here and see what
          a mess you been --

He stops suddenly as one of the guys turns and he sees his face. Big ass
demon. We'll call him DEMON 1.

Demon 1 smiles as DEMON 2 picks up an ARM IN FLANNEL SHIRT, still clutching
a 9mm auto pistol, and drops it into the burning drum. (They're in the
process of getting rid of what's left of Gang Banger's buddies.)

And now we SEE the FACES of DEMON 2 and DEMON 3. They look just like Demon
1. And when they smile they reveal their double rows of shark-like teeth.
(Or something to that effect.)

Gang Banger suddenly turns and runs. And the three demons go after him.

3 EXT. STREET - NIGHT

Gang Banger tears out from under the bridge, racing down the street as fast
as he can. Pulls a gun from the back of his pants.

The three demons chase. Gaining on Gang Banger.

Gang Banger, terrified, fires wildly at them as he runs. He races across a street. Continuing to fire wildly until his gun is empty.

He glances back over his shoulder. And they're now only twenty feet behind him. And they're smiling.

Gang Banger tries to run faster.

The three demons are enjoying the chase. Not tired at all. But suddenly they are lit from behind... by a CAR'S HEADLIGHTS. Coming up fast.

THE DEMONS

annoyed, turn around to look just as the BLADE OF A SWORD slices off ALL THEIR HEADS. They drop and we --

SEE ANGEL'S CONVERTIBLE

roar past. Top down. Angel is holding the sword and Wesley is driving.

The car races ahead of the running Gang Banger, Wesley putting it into a skid. It spins around, screeches to a stop in front of Gang Banger, illuminating him in the headlights. The Gang Banger stops, exhausted. Staring into the headlights, not sure whether he will live or die.

ANGEL STEPS INTO THE HEADLIGHTS, SILHOUETTING HIM. Still holding the big bloody sword.

                    ANGEL
          Your name Marquez?

Gang Banger nods.

                    ANGEL (cont'd)
          Good. I hate saving the wrong guy.

Suddenly we HEAR AN UNEARTHLY GROWL. Angel spins around, wielding the sword.

The Gang Banger is wide-eyed and terrified. Frozen stiff with fear as we HEAR (all off screen action) THE SWORD CONNECT with FLESH AND BONE. We HEAR the fall of a body, the THUMP of a HEAD. And possibly get a splash of white, pus-like blood as it splatters. Angel turns back to Marquez.

                    ANGEL (cont'd)
          Never know who you're gonna meet in this part of
          town. Want a ride?

4 EXT. BUS DEPOT - THE BAD PART OF TOWN - NIGHT

The BUS DEPOT in downtown. It's dark, late. Streets empty. A GREYHOUND TYPE BUS pulls into the depot.

5 INT. BUS DEPOT GARAGE - NIGHT

CLOSE ON BUS DOORS as they HISS OPEN and a FEW LEGS exit. Some sneakers with baggy pants, pumps with an old dress, and black boots with jeans. We FOLLOW THE BLACK BOOTS AND JEANS as they move toward the exit.

6 EXT. BUS DEPOT - NIGHT

A LIGHTED MATCH touches the end of a cigarette and is drawn in as somebody sucks the flame into the leaves. And we FOLLOW the flow to the thin lips of a somewhat handsome man in his thirties. He's wearing a leather jacket, a couple of gold chains. We'll call him DICK. But his attention is on...

...the jeans that have just walked out of the bus depot. From here we can tell it's a slender woman... with dark hair. She's carrying a battered bag. Her hair is across her face, so we can't get a good look at her. She looks a bit ragged. Maybe it's from the long bus trip. There seems to be some hesitation. As if she's new in the city and not sure of her directions.

BUT AS SHE TURNS AND STARTS WALKING TOWARD US, WE SEE IT'S FAITH. She looks like she hasn't slept for a week and has been living on black coffee. And walking an emotional tight rope for too long.

Dick's thin lips curl into a smile as he waits for the woman. He blows out smoke and sucks it back up into his nose.

Faith passes right past Dick without a look. Dick moves out, right behind her.

                    DICK
          New in town, right? You got that new in town look.
          Dangerous part of town this time of night for a
          young lady... by herself.

Faith keeps walking. Dick moves up, walking side by side with her.

                    DICK (cont'd)
          Lot a people down here try'n take advantage of a
          situation like that. Especially if you don't have
          any money... or a place to stay...

Faith looks at Dick through the hair that falls across her face. She makes no attempt to brush it aside, as if she doesn't notice. And she doesn't stop walking. Dick smiles. Trying to project a friendly, nice guy image.

                    DICK (cont'd)
          I might be able to help.

                    FAITH
          I'm cold.

Dick's got her now.

                    DICK
          Warm is my middle name.

Dick takes off his leather jacket and when it's half way down his arms --

Faith suddenly throws an elbow, smashing Dick in the face. He is stunned. Faith grabs him and slams against the building. And she's on him, hitting him again and again. A little over the top considering Dick's arms are still caught up in his coat half way down his back. He can't even lift a hand in defense.

Dick slams face first to the ground. Out. Then she kneels down on his back, yanks his wallet from his pocket. Opens it.

                    FAITH
          Now I got money.
          (pulls out his keys)
          And a place to stay.

She pulls off his leather jacket, slips it on. Good fit. She brushes her hair back, looks at the bleakness around her.

                    FAITH (cont'd)
          I think I'm gonna like it here.

BLACK OUT.

                    END OF TEASER

                    ACT ONE

SUPER LEGEND: Borsa, Rumania, 1890s.

7 INT. HOUSE - RUMANIA - NIGHT (FLASHBACK)

The interior of the house and the furniture hopefully tells us we're in the eighteen hundreds. The room is lit by lanterns. It's dim and shadowy inside. The door suddenly opens and Angel, dressed in the attire of old, stumbles in, blindfolded.

He stumbles, but catches himself. Is he a captive?

Angel starts to laugh as he stands up and turns back to the door just as Darla enters, pushing the door shut. She's smiling.

                    ANGEL
          Can I take off this damn blindfold yet?

                    DARLA
          No.

Darla starts to walk past him, but Angel grabs her and pulls her to him. His hand pressing against the small of her back.

                    ANGEL
          Then can I take off something else?

Darla smiles.

                    DARLA
          After I give you your present.

He pulls her into a kiss. She lets him have his way for a moment, then she pushes away from him, laughing.

                    DARLA (cont'd)
          You can never have enough of these.

She grabs his hand and pulls him along. Angel tries not to stumble.

                    DARLA (cont'd)
               Come on.
8 INT. DARLA'S HOUSE - DINING ROOM - NIGHT

A fire crackles in the large stone fireplace. Darla drags Angel into the room. She positions him. Then moves behind him and undoes his blindfold.

P.O.V. AS THE BLINDFOLD IS REMOVED

REVEALING a BEAUTIFUL SEVENTEEN YEAR OLD GYPSY GIRL lying on the floor. Hands and feet chained tightly. Her mouth gagged. She is terrified.

                    DARLA
          Happy birthday, Angelus.

By the look on Angel's face we can tell he likes the present.

                    ANGEL
          She's a Gypsy.

                    DARLA
          I looked _every_where.

Angel looks at Darla.

                    ANGEL
          What would I do without you?

                    DARLA
          Wither and die.

Angel pulls Darla into a passionate kiss. Then, as they part, Darla looks
into his eyes and smiles.

                    DARLA (cont'd)
          She's not just for you. I get to watch.

Angel smiles. Then he lets go of Darla, turns to the terrified young woman.

The young gypsy woman's eyes widen in fear as Angel approaches.

Angel reaches down for her and MORPHS to vamp. The woman tries to scream,
but the sound is muffled by her gag.

Angel sensuously moves a hand up her bare leg, slowly pushing up her skirt
above her knee, up her thigh.

Angel smiles at her. Then he slowly moves down to her leg and sinks his
teeth into the inside of her thigh... just above the knee, get your mind out
of the gutter.

Darla watches. Almost as if she can feel her own teeth sinking into Angelus.

9 INT. ANGEL'S OUTER OFFICE - DAY

The door is closed to Angel's office. Cordy is at the door trying to hear
what's going on inside. Wes is pacing.

                    CORDELIA
          -- This guy's never gonna do it. What a waste of a
          good vision.

                    WESLEY
          It's going that badly?

                    CORDELIA
          I knew it when you brought him in last night.
          Someone with that much body art is going to have a
          different definition of civic duty.

Wesley looks distressed.

                    WESLEY
          After we saved his life?!

                CORDELIA
When was the last time you wrote a thank you card?

                WESLEY
Well I have faith in Angel. If anyone can convince
him to testify --

                CORDELIA
-- Wesley, you don't change a guy like that. In
fact, generally speaking, you don't change a guy.
What you see is what you get. Scratch the surface
and what do you find? More surface.

                WESLEY
Well I suppose one could have said that about...
Angel.

                CORDELIA
Oh, please, he was cursed by gypsies. What's Angel
going to do, drag a bunch of them in here to shove
a soul down this guy's throat?

                WESLEY
He may be a ruffian, but he's already got a soul --
and therefore, somewhere deep down inside, an urge
to do what's right.

Suddenly the office door opens and Gang Banger is headed out--

                GANG BANGER
No way! I'm gone!

Angel grabs him and pulls him back into the office, slamming the door. Cor
looks at Wes:

                    CORDELIA
          I guess you're right, Wes, he's just like the Dalai
          Lama.

10 INT. ANGEL'S INNER OFFICE - DAY

Angel slams Gang Banger down into a chair and leans right down into his
face.

                    ANGEL
          The only way you're gonna keep from getting killed
          is to do the right thing!

                    GANG BANGER
          Right thing for who?!

Gang Banger tries to get up. Angel won't let him.

                    ANGEL
          Next time they come after you, I'm not gonna be
          there. And your friends aren't gonna be there
          either, not after being cut up and incinerated.

Beat.

                    ANGEL (cont'd)
          You don't even know what you're up against... Do
          you.

Angel is right. Gang Banger doesn't know what came after him last night.
And the fear is back.

                    ANGEL (cont'd)
          ...You're gonna have to face your demons sometime.

                    GANG BANGER
          What if I don't wanna face my demons.

                    ANGEL
          Then you'll have to face mine.

11 EXT. BAR - NIGHT - STOCK - ESTABLISHING

A FEW YOUNG FOLK showing ID'S to get in. Not that it matters. The MUSIC is
already LOUD. When the door opens, it's a jolt.

12 INT. BAR - NIGHT

The place is packed. Lots of black. It's dark. Strange lighting pulses.
Dance floor packed. In the middle of it all we see a woman who is in rock
and roll overdrive. As she spins around we see it's Faith. Lost in pounding
rhythms. Attracting the attention of SEVERAL MEN. She dances past a few to a
COUPLE.

The woman is VERY ATTRACTIVE. Faith smiles at the woman, starts dancing with
her man. The man isn't quite sure what to do about this, but it is clearly
what we call a luxury problem at this point.

The Attractive Woman is pissed.

                    ATTRACTIVE WOMAN
          Excuse me...

>   FAITH
>   Okay, you're excused.

Faith wraps her arms around guy's neck, dancing dirty close now. Attractive
Woman grabs Faith, pulling her around.

>   ATTRACTIVE WOMAN
>   That's my boyfriend.

>   FAITH
>   Really? Does he have your name on him?

Faith peeks down guy's shirt.

>   FAITH (cont'd)
>   I don't see it... anywhere...

>   ATTRACTIVE WOMAN
>   (to boyfriend, furious)
>   Billy, do something.

>   FAITH
>   Yeah Billy, do something... like this.

And Faith cracks her elbow back into Attractive's face, sending her
sprawling into another several dancers -- chain reaction of shoving and
anger starting as BILLY, at first shocked, then furious, swings at Faith who
gracefully ducks -- Billy hits another guy and the brawl is on.

And now fists and feet fly. With Faith in the middle of it. Enjoying her
carefree moment of violence, grabbing one guy, punching the hell out of him,
then slamming an elbow into someone else.

This is a major free-for-all. Faith is out of control. Unleashing herself on
everybody. AND ROCKIN' TO THE MUSIC.

13 INT. COURTROOM - DAY

TRIAL in progress. A handsome, rough-looking GUY, wearing a great suit, is
sitting at the defense table. He's the client. Next to him is LEE MERCER, a
Jr. lawyer at Wolfram and Hart. Both of them look confident.

A PROSECUTION ATTORNEY from the District Attorney's Office is at the
Prosecution table. No expression of confidence here. It's all he can do to
keep from burying his head in his hands.

The JUDGE and TWO ATTORNEYS are in the middle of a sidebar. And everyone is
waiting.

THE SIDEBAR AT THE BENCH

The Judge, ASSISTANT DISTRICT ATTORNEY and Lindsey.

>   LINDSEY
>   ...and while the arguments the District Attorney has
>   presented are somewhat entertaining, the case hinges
>   on testimony of witnesses they have been unable to
>   produce.

>   ASSISTANT D.A.
>   Your Honor, we could produce them if Wolfram and
>   Hart would stop tampering --

LINDSEY
Witness tampering is a serious allegation,
Counselor. And 1 will be filing a grievance for that
remark with the A.B.A. this afternoon.
(back to Judge)
They have no witness, they have no case. I request
a dismissal of all charges against my client, whose
reputation has been irreparably damaged by these
proceedings.

Judge nods, she has to agree. Suddenly the doors at the back of the
courtroom open. Lindsey, still speaking, turns to see:

LINDSEY (cont'd)
He is a law abiding and upstanding citizen.

GANG BANGER AND ANGEL

moving down the aisle, approaching the bench. Gang Banger still looks a
little unsure, but Angel is right behind him. There is no turning back.
Lindsey and Angel lock eyes.

ANGEL
Your client really is, except for that pesky drug
dealing and murder stuff.

ASSISTANT D.A.
(coolly)
Your Honor, the state calls Mr. Marquez.

Mr. Marquez is quickly ushered in.

THE DEFENDANT and MERCER - suddenly don't look so happy.

LINDSEY

looks back in time to see...

ANGEL

leaving the courtroom.

14 INT. WOLFRAM & HART - LINDSEY'S OFFICE - DAY

Lindsey is strolling around his office, speaking into his wireless telephone
headset.

LINDSEY
... No, sir, I accept full responsibility. I
thought we had done everything possible. However I
had not foreseen the intervention...

The door opens. Mercer sticks his head in. Lindsey waves him in and crosses
back.

LINDSEY (cont'd)
Yes, sir. Angel... I don't disagree. He is proving
to be a costly liability... I'll do that... Yes,
sir, good-bye.

LINDSEY TAKES OFF HIS HEAD PHONE WITH A SIGH.

                              LINDSEY (cont'd)
          I hate failure when there's no one else to blame it
          on.

                              MERCER
          I think I might have a solution to our problem.

Lindsey turns to Mercer, who pulls a page from his briefcase. Presenting it
with confidence.

A15 INT. WOLFRAM AND HART - DAY

MERCER moves down the hall, past the conference room. He becomes aware of a
TAPPING sound, looks over.

HIS POV - INSIDE THE CONFERENCE ROOM

And moving with him is LILAH, a few files in hand. Signaling she wants to
talk to him.

(NOTE: if we don't have a conference room that supports this visual, we can
just have Mercer moving down a hall and find Lilah moving up behind him --
in that version she'd say, "Lee, I've been looking for you," then turn to
the lawyer she's walking with and deliver her first line "drop dead offer"
before turning her attention to Mercer.)

As they meet at the doorway, she turns back and says to one of the LAWYERS
in the room:

                              LILAH
          Call them back and tell them that's our drop dead
          offer -- and make sure they undertand we're speaking
          literally not figuratively.
          (to Mercer)
          How are you doing?

                              MERCER
          Good. You?

                              LILAH
          Great. I hear you came up with a good idea.
          (off his look)
          To deal with our friendly neighborhood vampire.

                              MERCER
          No, I came up with a great idea. How do you find
          these things out so fast?

                              LILAH
          Part of my job. How did you find out there was a
          rogue slayer in town?

                              MERCER
          Part of my job -- I read the police reports, she's
          been a busy little beaver.

                              LILAH
          But you don't know where she is.

                              MERCER
          I will soon enough.

                    LILAH
          I already do.

Lilah shows him one of the files in her hand. He reaches for it, she pulls
it back.

                    LILAH (cont'd)
          I'll make the contact.

                    MERCER
          I don't think so, this is my deal. I'll make the
          contact.

                    LILAH
          Let me think about that --
          (almost instantly:)
          -- no.

                    MERCER
          Why not?

                    LILAH
          It's your people skills --
          you don't have any.

                    MERCER
          You bitch.

                    LILAH
          See?
          (moving off)
          Don't have a snit -- if
          you behave, I'll let you
          ride in the limo.

FLASHY CUT TO:

B15 INT. ANGEL'S OFFICE - DAY

Cordelia is on the phone.

                    CORDELIA
          I'm terribly sorry about your
          wife cheating on you, Mr. Garson,
          but we don't really handle
          divorce...
          (listens:)
          ...she slept with the dog?
          (listens more:)
          Oh, Shiatsu, not Shih-tzu -- she slept with the
          masseur -- which isn't good, either.

(PRODUCTION NOTE: Shiatsu is pronounced SHE OUGHT SUE, emphasis on middle
syllable OUGHT. Shih-tzu is pronounced SHEET SUE.)

                    CORDELIA (cont'd)
          But unfortunately we don't really do divorce
          cases...
          (listens)
          ...no, it's not about the money...
          (listens some more)
          ...oh, it's about that much money... how soon can we
          meet?

As Cor writes down an address, we pan or dolly to Angel's office door as Angel and Wesley step out of Angel's elevator.

> CORDELIA (O.S.)
> ...I know where that is. We'll be there tomorrow, thanks for calling, bye.

They bring us back to her as she hangs up.

> CORDELIA
> How'd it go?

> WESLEY
> We won.

> CORDELIA
> Gang guy testified?

> ANGEL
> Stood up and told the truth.

> CORDELIA
> (to Wesley)
> What did I tell you.

> WESLEY
> That he never would.

> CORDELIA
> (ignores that)
> More good news, I may have landed a new client -- and here's a twist: he can afford to pay.

> WESLEY
> What's the case?

> CORDELIA
> (evasive)
> I'm still in the information gathering phase... we're meeting him for lunch tomorrow.
> (to Angel, to change subject)
> So are you happy with the way things turned out?

Angel nods, deep in his own thoughts.

> CORDELIA (cont'd)
> (to Wesley)
> You can always tell when he's happy. His scowl is slightly less scowly.

> WESLEY
> That young man is lucky he ran into you.

> ANGEL
> He just needed a little guidance, a push in the right direction.

> WESLEY
> I wonder how Wolfram and Hart are going to push back?

A beat. All three of them worried about that now.

CORDELIA
Did I mention our new paying client?

15 EXT. ANOTHER BAR - NIGHT

LOUD MUSIC gushing into the street. A FEW BARFLIES enter as Faith exits with
an attractive WOMAN. We may not see her face at first, just concentrate on
Faith, who is a bit wobbly. (NOTE TO DIRECTOR AND ACTORS: Mind the lesbian
subtext -- keep it very "sub".)

                    FAITH
          ... I guess we could go somewhere and talk...
          although I'm not much of a talker... I'm more of a
          doer.

                    WOMAN
          I think you might've misunderstood my intentions.

We see the woman now. It's LILAH, from Wolfram and Hart. She stops walking.
Faith stops with her, staring at her and leaning in close, backing her
against a wall.

                    FAITH
          No. I think you misunderstood mine. I like that
          watch. Diamonds, right?

                    LILAH
          Faith --

                    FAITH
          How'd you know my name?

Faith puts her hands against the wall, one on either side of Lilah's neck.

                    FAITH (cont'd)
          I don't think I told you.

Lilah is not liking this.

                    LILAH
          We're well aware of who you are and what you do.
          And we know that you're experiencing some
          difficulties. We think we can help bring a little
          more order to your life.

Faith pushes right up against Lilah --

                    FAITH
          "We" do, do we? Who is "we" and why do they know
          about me when I don't know jack about you?

And just as Faith is about to unleash --

                    LILAH
          Green is my favorite color, I look good in diamonds,
          and I love riding in limousines.

A LONG BLACK LIMOUSINE

...slides up. Door opening. Faith turns at the sound, ready to hurt something. But Mercer sticks his head out. He's dressed in a sharp Armani.

                              MERCER
                    Faith...

Faith doesn't know what the hell is going on.

                              MERCER (cont'd)
                    ...can we talk?

Mercer disappears back into the limo. Faith hesitates a beat, then looks at
Lilah.

                              FAITH
                    I like black.

Faith gets into the back. Lilah breathes a sigh of relief, then gets in.
The door shuts.

The limo tears off down the street.

BLACK OUT.

                         <u>END OF ACT ONE</u>

                           <u>ACT TWO</u>

16 INT. DARLA'S HOUSE - NIGHT (FLASHBACK)

The door opens and Darla enters.

                              DARLA
                    Angelus.

She moves through the House.

                              DARLA (cont'd)
                    Are you here?

17 INT. LIVING ROOM - NIGHT (FLASHBACK)

DARLA enters. The room is dark, there may be a candle or two burning.

                              DARLA
                    Angelus --

THERE IS MOVEMENT IN THE SHADOWS AT THE BACK OF THE ROOM.

Darla turns quickly... not sure if she's in danger.

                              ANGEL
                    Not everyone screams...

                              DARLA
                    What...?

                              ANGEL
                    ...when you kill them. Some just stand there,
                    frozen, while others...

She recognizes his voice. But he's still in the shadows. As if he's hiding.

                              DARLA
                    What are you doing? Are we playing a game?

Angel steps out of the shadows now. Self-consciously. And when we see him we know why. He looks terrible, like he's been hit by a runaway carriage pulled by four stallions.

                    ANGEL
          ...the children, they usually scream...

Darla thinks about this for a moment. Remembering it as a pleasant experience.

                    DARLA
          They sound just like little pigs.

She smiles with anticipation.

                    DARLA (cont'd)
          Have you brought me some?

Nothing from Angel.

                    DARLA (cont'd)
          What, you don't think I'll share? I can't believe
          you think I'm that insensitive.

                    ANGEL
          We've drunk and killed for how long now...? A
          hundred and forty odd years? We've drunk them all up
          and they're all dead...

He laughs a little at that (maybe). It's not a sane laugh.

                    DARLA
          Where have you been...?

For the first time, Darla gets the sense that something is really wrong with Angel. Like a woman whose radar has just picked up her man's cheatin' heart. She knows something has changed, but she's not sure what.

Angel leans against the wall, half curled up, as if trying to will himself to disappear or die.

She moves closer. Reaching to touch him.

                    ANGEL
          Don't...

                    DARLA
          What is this?! Have you met someone else?

He closes his eyes, struggling with the visions for a moment,
then he moves to her, putting his arms around her.

She starts to put her arms around him, but suddenly she is overcome with revulsion. She tries to push away from him.

                    DARLA (cont'd)
          NO... Let go... *Let go of me!*

Darla bursts back from him as if an invisible force suddenly separates them.

                    DARLA (cont'd)
          What's happened to you?!

Angel hesitates, desperate, not knowing how to tell her --

                    DARLA (cont'd)
          ANGELUS! What happened?!

                         ANGEL
          That Gypsy girl you brought, her people found out,
          they did something to me...

                         DARLA
          A spell.

                         ANGEL
          Funny, you'd think with all the people I've maimed
          and killed I wouldn't be able to remember every
          single one... help me.

She stares at him, then slowly reaches out, touches his face. A flicker of
hope in his eyes, as:

                         DARLA
          The spell... they gave you a soul...

He nods. And suddenly she drags her hand down his face, leaving three or so
long bloody marks. He leaps back.

                    DARLA (cont'd)
          ...a filthy soul.

From here on out she is filled with a growing repulsion and horror -- just
like a normal person would be in the presence of a vampire.

                    DARLA (cont'd)
          No! You're disgusting.

Angel is stunned.

                         ANGEL
          Darla...

                         DARLA
          Get away from me.

                         ANGEL
          You brought her here!

Darla suddenly picks up a chair and flings it against the wall. Her power is
stunning. The chair shatters. But she retains a broken piece of the chair
leg - a stake.

And she swipes at him. He barely escapes it. Darla starts toward him again.
He backs away.

                    ANGEL (cont'd)
          I am like you!

                         DARLA
          You're not like anything. GET AWAY FROM ME!!

Darla lunges again. Angel dives under the stake or over a table and
stumbles out the door.

HER P.O.V. OF ANGEL OUTSIDE

206

Stumbling to his feet, turning around. Looking at her one last time... A mixture of confusion and hate... before he disappears into the shadows.

18 INT. WOLFRAM & HART'S OFFICE - NIGHT

Faith is pacing like a caged animal. Moving around the office as if she's working out her options; steal something, break something, or kill somebody - where do I start?

Mercer, Lilah, and Lindsey are watching her as they proceed with the interview.

>   LINDSEY
>   (reading from a.p.b.)
>   ... where a felony arrest warrant from Sunnydale was
>   issued in your name...
>   (impressed)
>   ... for murder.
>   (looks Faith)
>   The physical description is quite accurate. The
>   photograph, however, is not flattering. There's lots
>   of personal stuff that's of no interest. But what
>   they fail to mention is... you're a slayer.

Faith turns to face them. Not sure if she should attack or make for the door.

>   LILAH
>   Which is why we find you especially appealing.

>   LINDSEY
>   (stands up; paces)
>   You have a problem. We have a problem. I just had a
>   perfectly good murder case go up in smoke, you seem
>   to have a certain expertise in that area yourself.
>   So, to make a long story less long, if a certain
>   service is rendered, I think we can get you off.

>   FAITH
>   You don't know how many men have promised me that.

>   LILAH
>   (laughs)
>   I'm certain you won't be disappointed with our
>   performance.

>   FAITH
>   Who am I supposed to kill?

Lindsey looks at Faith with a hopeful smile. Then sits back on his desk.

>   LINDSEY
>   Please understand, we would never advocate the
>   killing of any *human being*. His name is Angel.

Faith registers the name subtly.

>   LINDSEY (cont'd)
>   He's somewhat of a private --

>   FAITH
>   -- no problem.

Everyone is a little surprised by quick acceptance. She's almost a little
too eager.

>   MERCER
>   Don't you want to know anything more?

>   FAITH
>   Yeah. Besides gettin' me off, how much you gonna
>   pay?

>   MERCER
>   It might behoove you to know a little more about
>   your intended.
>   (approaches her)
>   So before we discuss remuneration --

>   FAITH
>   (pointedly)
>   -- huh?

>   MERCER
>   ...Payment... I want to make sure you understand
>   that this firm is in no way connected to anything
>   you do.

Mercer moves up to her, leans in.

>   MERCER (cont'd)
>   It's my ass on the line here. I don't want you to
>   make me look bad.

Faith looks at him for half a beat, then with unbelievable speed she takes
him by the hair and slams his head into an antique or other interesting
table...

>   FAITH
>   How do you look now?

As she continues to pound his head into the table (we should probably only
see the first slam) --

Lindsey and Lilah watch passively. Impressed by her ability and
ruthlessness.

>   LILAH
>   She shows initiative.

>   LINDSEY
>   (hits speaker-phone)
>   Jesse, I think we better make it
>   three for dinner instead of four.

19 INT. GOVERNMENT BUILDING ROTUNDA - DAY

Cordelia, Wesley and Angel walking through the Rotunda. Several people in
business attire entering and exiting.

>   CORDELIA
>   ...And he's kind of a busy man so lunch was the
>   only time he had.

>   CORDELIA (cont'd)
>   It's not the kind of case I would normally go

after, but we've got to consider the bottom line.

                    ANGEL
          What kind of demons are we dealing with?

                    CORDELIA
          Well, it's not exactly a demon thing.

                    WESLEY
          What kind of thing is it?

                    CORDELIA
          It's a... kind of... husband and wife break-up
          thing.

                    WESLEY
          A divorce case?

Angel stops.

                    ANGEL
          You're kidding.

                    CORDELIA
          (innocently incensed)
          What's wrong with a divorce case?

                    ANGEL
          It's not what we do.

                    CORDELIA
          According to the husband...
          (trying to sell it)
          ...the wife's a real witch.

                    WESLEY
          It seems a bit on the seedy side.

                    CORDELIA
          This is not seedy. He's in government!

Wesley and Angel give her a look.

                    CORDELIA (cont'd)
          Just talk to him. Oh, and we should pick up the
          tab for lunch.

                    CORDELIA (cont'd)
          Nothing says success less than splitting the bill.

                    ANGEL
          I didn't bring any money with me.

                    CORDELIA
          Okay, _Elvis_, when you're a big star you can get
          away without carrying cash.

ANGLE - ANGEL IN WIDE SINGLE

As Faith, unseen by all of them, suddenly appears behind him, moving up
fast.

CORDELIA (cont'd)
          And while we're on the subject, I think one of us
          should apply for a small business loan.

ANGLE - ABOVE LOOKING DOWN ON FAITH AND ANGEL

As she raises a large crossbow, aims it at his back. She's maybe six feet or
less behind him.

                    CORDELIA (cont'd)
          Just to get us through the rough spots.
          (to Angel)
          I mean, what's a thirty year loan to you?

FAITH - fires!

ANGEL

Spins around so quickly we hardly see the move, grabbing the arrow a
centimeter from entering his chest.

And he, Cordy and Wesley are stunned to find themselves staring at --

                    FAITH
          That was so cool.

BEFORE ANGEL CAN RESPOND, FAITH SAYS --

                    FAITH (cont'd)
          This is gonna be fun.

-- AS SHE TURNS AND RUNS, disappearing quickly out the exit.

                    WESLEY
          Oh... my God. Faith...

                    ANGEL
          I thought she was in a coma.

                    CORDELIA
          Pretty lively coma.

20 INT. ANGEL'S OFFICE - DAY

Angel hangs up the phone. Turns to face Wesley and Cordelia.

                    ANGEL
          Giles said she left Sunnydale about a week ago. He
          described her mental state as borderline psychotic.

                    CORDELIA
          That explains the outfit.

                    WESLEY
          This isn't right --

                    CORDELIA
          No, Wesley, when a wacked out Slayer tries to kill
          your boss, it's very wrong.

                    WESLEY
          I meant Giles. Why didn't he give me a heads up? I
          was Faith's Watcher; when she came out of her coma

210

Giles should have contacted me immediately.

CORDELIA
Maybe he was too busy trying to keep her from, I
don't know, killing everybody.

ANGEL
He didn't know she was coming after me... and he
was worried about Buffy.

CORDELIA
Is she okay?

ANGEL
Yeah.

Beat. Cordy knows Buffy is still a hard subject for Angel.

CORDELIA
What can we do?

ANGEL
Help me track her down. I
want you two to check police
reports, heatings, killings,
anything within the last week,
probably near bus stations and
bars. And then you make
yourselves scarce. I don't
want to give her any free
targets.

WESLEY
You've been targeted
by a psychotic. I'm
certainly not
going to run and
hide.

CORDELIA
I like the plan where I'm
scarce.

WESLEY
We've got to band together.
Strength in numbers.

CORDELIA
(indicating the men)
Two is a number.

ANGEL
She's coming for me. I got a fight coming up and I
don't want you getting in the way.

WESLEY
(stung)
I thought we were a team.

ANGEL
We're not a team. I'm your boss. You go where I
tell you and I tell you to lay low.

                    WESLEY
          Seems you're taking this personally.

                    ANGEL
          She tried to shoot my own personal back, so yeah.

                    WESLEY
          Did she do something to Buffy?

Angel pauses.

                    ANGEL
          Giles just said it was rough.

                    WESLEY
          I'm sorry. But if you let your emotion control you
          right now one of you will certainly end up dead.

                    ANGEL
          That's what the lady wants...

                    WESLEY
          (a bit in his face)
          That's not good enough. She's not a demon. Angel.
          She's a sick, sick girl. If there's even a chance
          she could be reasoned with --

                    ANGEL
          There was. Last year I had a shot at saving her, I
          was pulling her back from the brink when some
          British guy kidnapped her and made damn sure she'd
          never trust another living soul.

                    CORDELIA
          Angel, it's not Wesley's fault some British guy
          ruined your -- oh wait.
          (to Wes)
          That was you.
          (to Angel)
          Go on.

                    WESLEY
          (a bit downcast)
          You don't need to.

A moment, as Angel wants to say something, can only offer:

                    ANGEL
          Let's get to work.

21 EXT. LOS ANGELES SKYLINE - DAY (STOCK)

JUMP CUTTY TRANSITION, maybe involving weapons. Faith, to:

22 INT. ANGEL'S APARTMENT - DAY

A cabinet opens. Revealing an impressive array of strange weapons.

Angel looks them over, making his decision.

We HEAR SOMETHING from upstairs. Nothing too obvious. Just enough to make
one wonder if he should take a look. But it could be just Wes or Cordy

coming back for something.

23 INT. ANGEL'S OFFICE - DAY

Angel enters slowly. Nobody appears to be inside. He moves through the office. Not sure if he's just being overly cautious... He stops, sensing a presence. We hear blinds... He turns quickly...

...Through the open door to the outer office, the blinds on Cordelia's window open, sun flooding in.

                    FAITH
          Hey, baby.

Faith steps into the bright sunlight.

                    FAITH (cont'd)
          Come give us a hug.

                    ANGEL
          I was hoping you'd stop by. I always like to see
          old friends.

Faith pulls a snub nose revolver from behind her back.

                    ANGEL (cont'd)
          What's this, wooden bullets?

                    FAITH
          Oooo, good idea. No, it's for you. I got a sense of
          fair play -- you know I'll kill you slowly and
          inventively -- so I'm giving you one chance to --

She tosses him the gun on the word "chance". But the word "to" he is already FIRING THE GUN (at her leg).

The SOUND INSIDE THE OFFICE is deafening.

Faith looks down at her leg. She looks up at Angel with a smile. Like she's enjoying it. On a high.

                    ANGEL
          Blanks? Nice.

Angel tosses the gun back to Faith.

                    FAITH
          Tsk, tsk, you didn't shoot to kill. We're gonna have
          to up the stakes, get you in the game a little.

                    ANGEL
          What is the game, exactly, Faith? Boredom, revenge?

                    FAITH
          Dude, I'm gettin' paid!

                    FAITH (cont'd)
          They hate you almost as much as I do.

                    ANGEL
          Did it ever occur to you this might be more fun for
          me?

Faith steps out of the light toward Angel.

> FAITH
> Ya think? 'Cause what if you kill me and experience
> that one true moment of pleasure? Oops. I'd get off
> on that. Go 'head, do me. Let's take that hell ride
> together.

For the first time Angel gets a real sense of how far gone she really is.

> FAITH (cont'd)
> Come on Angel, I'm all yours. I'm givin' you an
> open invitation.

Angel hesitates.

> FAITH (cont'd)
> Jeez, you're pathetic, you and your little tortured
> soul, gotta think everything through -- well think
> fast, lover, you don't do me, you know I'm gonna do
> you.

She suddenly aims the gun at him. Faith pulls the trigger. Angel is slammed
with a bullet. He looks up, surprised. But no surprise for Faith.

> FAITH (cont'd)
> Gosh, that one wasn't a blank -- let the games
> begin.

Faith smiles and leaps for the window. CRASHING THROUGH IT INTO THE SUN-
LIGHT. THE SUDDEN LIGHT blows the screen WHITE as we --

24 EXT. WOLFRAM & HART LAW OFFICE - NIGHT - STOCK - ESTABLISH

25 INT. WOLFRAM & HART'S LOBBY - NIGHT

Lindsey is leaving. Looks like he's done for the day. Chatting for a sec
with another young lawyer BRET FOLGER.

                        LINDSEY
        ...it's a situation we're handling.

                        BRET
        I saw the file -- he needs to be handled. Gotta
        jump.

Bret intercepts another passing Lawyer, Lindsey moves off. We follow Lindsey
BUT HOLD ON A BRIEFCASE WHICH SUDDENLY FILLS FRAME moving the other way. (In
such a way that Lindsey would NOT have seen Angel, obviously.)

ANGLE ON BRIEFCASE as it's carried past a FEW PEOPLE calling it a day. We
HEAR some "See you tomorrow"s and "Have a good night"s as we PAN UP TO
REVEAL ANGEL. He's wearing a suit, carrying the briefcase. Looking rather
sharp and lawyer-esque. Hey, let's not comb his hair any different.

ANGEL MOVES PAST THE SECURITY DESK. The SECURITY OFFICER, who is in the
midst of converstaion with a DELIVERY MAN, pays no attention.

Then suddenly Angel sees Bret Folger heading right towards him, staring hard
at his face.

                        BRET (cont'd)
        You...
        (tense beat)
        ...were in the Gruber meeting.

                        ANGEL
        Right.

                        BRET
        What the hell is going on with those people?

                        ANGEL
        I know, it's, uh...

                        BRET
        I mean is this a negotiation or a cotillion?

                        ANGEL
        That's exactly what I was saying to, uh, Frank --

                        BRET
        Who's Frank?

                        ANGEL
        Works with Louisa in contracts.

                        BRET
        The problem is not contracts!

                        ANGEL
        Which I tried to tell Frank, but --

Bret's cell phone rings. He holds up his hand to silence Angel, takes the
call.

                    BRET
          (into phone)
          Go... yes, yes, no... Thursday.
          (clicks off; to Angel)
          We have to close Gruber now before the soft offer
          becomes hard and the stock goes --
          (gestures a little wildly)

                    ANGEL
          Through the ceil --

                    BRET
          In the toilet.

                    ANGEL
          Right.

                    BRET
          Keep me in the loop, I want to know the instant
          they fold -- they are folding...?

Angel makes "fuhhh" sound -- of course they're folding.

                    BRET (cont'd)
          Right. Gotta jump. E-mail me. Good to see you.

                    ANGEL
          (to Bret's departing back)
          You, too.

Angel glides into elevator.

26 INT. LINDSEY'S OFFICE - WOLFRAM & HART - NIGHT

Door opens. Angel enters. Shutting the door. The blinds are open on the
large floor to ceiling window. REVEALING L.A. at night. The office is empty.

Angel crosses to Lindsey's desk. Immediately starts going through the papers
on top. Searching the drawers.

He moves to the file cabinets behind the desk. Pulls open the top drawer,
continues the search.

The door opens. Angel looks up. Too late to hide.

Lindsey enters. Sees Angel. But there is no surprise in his expression.

                    LINDSEY
          Don't you have any respect for the law?

                    ANGEL
          Nice office. Good view. Where's Faith?

                    LINDSEY
          Should I know what you're talking about?

                    ANGEL
          Your new employee.

                    LINDSEY
          This is a big firm. I'll give you the number to
          personnel, I'm sure they'd be glad to handle your
          problem.

                    ANGEL
          You'd remember this one. Pretty, dark hair, kills
          things.

                    LINDSEY
          I assure you, we have strict hiring practices.

                    ANGEL
          So how's it work for a guy like you? Successful
          lawyer in a big law firm. Company car, nice office,
          bonus, can hire a killing whenever you want. Kind of
          got it made, right?

                    LINDSEY
          Well let's just add slander to breaking and
          entering. And while we're on the subject, I
          remember you throwing one of my clients through a
          window. Killed him if I'm not mistaken.

                    ANGEL
          ...Yes, I seem to remember...
          (looks at window)
          ...the window was just about that size.
          (looks at Lindsey)
          Too bad the body burned up before it hit the
          ground. I might have needed a good lawyer.

                    LINDSEY
          I'm sorry, we only handle a certain class of
          clientele.

                    ANGEL
          I'm sure I've killed enough people to qualify.

Angel starts toward Lindsey.

                    ANGEL (cont'd)
          Where is she?

                    LINDSEY
          A vampire can't walk in here without us knowing
          about it. We have a highly sophisticated security
          system. We spent a fortune on mystical barriers and
          such. Nice to know our investment paid off.

Suddenly a LARGE SECURITY GUARD enters, behind Angel, gun drawn, coming up
fast. Angel never turns, never misses a beat in the conversation --

                    ANGEL
          I think it was a waste of money, myself.

Angel reaches behind and disarms Guard, slamming his head down onto the same
antique table that Faith beat Mercer's head against.

                    LINDSEY
          You know I just had that cleaned.

The table doesn't collapse as the guard drops to the floor unconscious.

                    ANGEL
          That's too bad.

> LINDSEY
> One down, more on the way. And the police have been
> called.

> LINDSEY (cont'd)
> And this whole encounter has been digitally recorded
> in Hi-Def. So, despite the fact that I'm sure it
> would be an entertaining evening watching you fight
> for your life, and I could make a fortune off the
> video, I do have a dinner.

Angel realizes his chance of obtaining the information he needs is slim.

> ANGEL
> Good to see you, Lindsey, we'll do this again soon.

Angel heads for the door.

> LINDSEY
> You know, just when I think I've got you figured
> out... you show up in a suit.

Angel exits. As the door closes --

27 INT. CORDELIA'S APARTMENT - HALL - NIGHT

Cor and Wes move down the hall. Wesley reading from some papers.

> WESLEY
> -- there's another assault just two blocks away. A
> fight in a bar. Several arrests made. And a woman
> fitting Faith's description was involved. However
> not arrested.

> CORDELIA
> She charm her way out?

> WESLEY
> (still reading)
> No, apparently she managed to break a policeman's
> jaw with his own handcuffs, before she disappeared
> into the night.

> CORDELIA
> For Faith, that *is* charm.

She unlocks her door.

A28 INT. CORDELIA'S APARTMENT - NIGHT

Cordelia opens the door -- or tries to -- it is suddenly shoved back closed.
She pushes it open, battling an unseen force. She struggles with the door:

> CORDELIA
> Phantom Dennis! Let us in -- it's all right, it's
> only Wesley.

She shoves the door open and they enter. Wes carries some papers.

> WESLEY
> Dennis, your ghost, I presume.

> CORDELIA
> He's a little jealous.
> (to the air, re: Wesley)
> Don't worry, hell will freeze over before I have sex
> with him.

> WESLEY
> (to himself)
> Thank goodness for small favors.
> (re: papers)
> I'll try calling Angel again.

> CORDELIA
> I'll pack a bag.

28 OMITTED

A28 CONTINUED:

> WESLEY
> Cordelia, please, just some basics. We're not going
> on safari.

> FAITH
> I got a little problem...

Cordelia, startled, turns quickly to find Faith stepping out of the shadows right behind her.

> FAITH (cont'd)
> I don't feel Angel's in the game.

Cordelia gives Wesley a look that says "We're in deep shit."

> FAITH (cont'd)
> But somehow, I think you guys are the key. Now what
> could I do to really make him hate me... hmmm?

> WESLEY
> Faith...

> FAITH
> Shut up, Wesley.

Wesley steps forward, making the man in charge move.

> WESLEY
> Listen to me, it's not too late.

> FAITH
> For cappuccino? 'Cause they keep me up.

> WESLEY
> It's not too late to let me help you.

Cordy glares at Wes, then backs up, eyes peeled, or hands searching, for a weapon.

> CORDELIA
> Yes, we want to help you.

Wesley continues on his uncharted course of take charge, be firm, yet compassionate.

                    WESLEY
          I realize there have been failures... on both sides.
          But, I also believe in my heart you are not a bad
          person.

Faith smiles, touched. Then she throws a round house and decks Cordelia. She
falls unconscious onto the floor. Wesley is stunned.

                    FAITH
          (friendly)
          What do you believe in your heart now?

Wesley suddenly lashes out and hits Faith hard in the jaw. Her head jerks to
one side with the blow. She's a little surprised, but she smiles.

                    FAITH (cont'd)
          (impressed)
          All right, Wes.
          (then)
          My turn --

Faith kicks, connects with Wesley's chest, sending him flying back into the
living room. And as Faith goes after him --

BLACK OUT.

                         END OF ACT TWO

                         ACT THREE

29 EXT. ALLEY - RUMANIA - NIGHT (FLASHBACK)

The alley is dark. Narrow. Muddy. A PAIR OF LATE NINETEENTH CENTURY SHOES
moves down the alley. Through the muck and pools of dark water, over the
partially visible skeleton of a dog. No attempt at trying to stay clean.

We PAN UP and see it's Angel, long hair down, desperation in the eyes, face
drawn, unshaven. His once nice clothes dirty and in disarray.

We HEAR SOUNDS of MUSIC. PERHAPS some lively folk songs filtering out from
inside like Liszt's Hungarian stuff. The pace of the walker slows down. We
HEAR VOICES... and DISTANT THUNDER.

30 EXT. RUMANIAN STREET - NIGHT (FLASHBACK)

A tavern on a corner, next to the dark alley. The TAVERN HAS A HANGING SIGN
WITH THE Rumanian equivalent of the 01' Hog's Head or the King's Arms. A
PRETTY TWENTYISH WOMAN, bundled up against the cold night, is exiting the
tavern with THREE MEN. They're laughing, having a grand ol' time. One of
the men puts his arm around the woman as they all start down the street
together.

ANGEL STEPS out of the alley, into the yellowish light cast from tavern windows. He looks like a man who's been on the run for awhile, but his expression is hard, angry, brooding. (The dialogue is a Slavic or Rumanian dialect
and subtitled.)

                    ANGEL
          ...Mie foame...
          (...I'm hungry...)

The men and woman are startled by Angel.

>   FIRST MAN
>   Pleaca de aici!
>   (Get away!)

The First Man moves toward Angel as if to strike him. The woman grabs his arm, holding him back.

>   THE WOMAN
>   Lasal in pace. E un cersetor.
>   (Let him be. He's just a beggar.)

First Man shakes his head, fishes a coin out of his pocket.
>   FIRST MAN
>   Bea o Bere.
>   (Have a pint on us.)
>   (flips coin to Angel)

Angel catches the coin in mid-air, <u>goading the men.</u>

>   ANGEL
>   Nu vreau banii rai...
>   (I don't want your money.)

The men look at him, surprised; Angel flings the coin back at the First Man, hard.

>   FIRST MAN
>   Ce ai spus!
>   (How dare you!)

Angel, suddenly a VAMP, looks up at them.

>   ANGEL
>   O vreau pe ea.
>   (I want her.)

Angel lunges for the Woman, who jumps back as First Man grabs his arm.

>   THE WOMAN
>   E un monstru!
>   (He's a monster!)

>   ANGEL
>   Eu sunt monstru.
>   (I'm a monster.)

>   FIRST MAN
>   Te omor.
>   (I'll kill you.)

And the men all attack Angel, driving him back into the alley as we PUSH IN on the startled woman. WE HEAR sounds of the terrible fight.

HER POV - ALLEY - Too dark to see what's happening in there.

After a beat, one of the men is flung out of the darkness and into the street, unconscious. Then silence. The woman doesn't know what to expect. As a dark figure, unrecognizable, moves out of the alley towards her:

                    THE WOMAN
          Rudolph? I esti bime?
          (Rudolph? Are you all right?)

But it is Angel, still in VAMP, not Rudolph, who steps out of the darkness.
The Woman screams, tries to run -- Angel grabs her lightning fast, pulls her
to him. The woman is terrified, Angel glares at her (we'll put an especially
vicious growl on the sound track) and shoves her hard -- harder than we've
ever seen him -- against the wall and overcoming whatever soul he might
have, sinks his fangs -- especially roughly -- into her neck.

31 INT. CORDELIA'S APARTMENT - NIGHT

RAINING OUTSIDE (or maybe no). The door is pushed open. It was unlocked.
Angel enters cautiously. Looks around the room. It's been trashed. Somebody
definitely got an ass kicked pretty damn hard in here.

                    ANGEL
          Cordy!

                    CORDELIA (O.S.)
          (weak)
          ...Angel.

He moves quickly into the -- DINING ROOM.

ANGEL ENTERS as Cordelia is slowly getting up off the floor, just having
regained consciousness. Angel helps her up.

                    CORDELIA
          She was already here. I didn't know. I made Wesley
          come with me...
          (trying to hide the guilt)
          ...just to get a couple things. And she was like an
          animal. She said you weren't in the game. There was
          nothing we could --

Cordelia loses control a bit, but trying not to. Angel attends to her.

                    ANGEL
          Take it easy.

                    CORDELIA
          -- I'm sorry.
          (looks up at Angel)
          What about Wesley. Is he okay?

                    ANGEL
          He's not here.

32 OMITTED

33 INT. DOWNTOWN LOFT APARTMENT - NIGHT

CLOSE ANGLE ON ROPES tied around Wesley's LEGS. CAMERA MOVING UP WESLEY'S
LEGS, AROUND THE CHAIR to his HANDS, TIED together, and CONTINUING UP TO A
KNOT behind his head, scarf pulled tight and stuffed in his mouth as a gag.
We HEAR BOOTS on HARDWOOD FLOOR. Walking slowly.

And we CONTINUE TO PULL BACK REVEALING WESLEY tied to a chair in the middle
of a large loft space. With Faith slowly circling.

Then she moves in close to him and sits down in his lap, straddling him, looking right into his eyes.   Putting her arms across his shoulders.

And now we see Wesley's face for the first time. It's already been bruised and cut from the battle in Cordelia's apartment.

Faith smiles. Licks her finger sensuously and seductively rubs a cut on the side of Wesley's face.

> FAITH
> All these little cuts and bruises just bring out the
> mother in me.

Suddenly Wesley's face is filled with pain. Gasping for air. She's obviously doing something to him that is not pleasant.

Faith gives it a moment, before she quits. Wesley is instantly relieved, eyes shut. Head nodding forward, breathing hard. She pushes his head back up.

> FAITH (cont'd)
> (a pep talk)
> Now now, don't poop out on me, dammit. Otherwise
> this is gonna be over way too fast. You'll be dead
> and I'll be bored.
> (one for the Gipper)
> Come on Wesley, where's the stiff upper lip?

Only now does one of Faith's hands reach below frame. Can't see what she's doing.

Faith gets off Wesley. Starts walking around him again.

> FAITH (cont'd)
> Now we've only done one of the five basic torture
> groups. We've had Blunt, but that still leaves
> Sharp, Cold, Hot and Loud. Have a preference?

A beat, then Wesley nods.

> FAITH (cont'd)
> Hey, great. It's always better with audience
> participation.

She undoes his gag.

> FAITH (cont'd)
> May I take your order please?

Wesley stares at her. And we get a sense that this guy is a lot stronger than we might have given him credit for.

> WESLEY
> I was your Watcher, Faith, I know the real you...
> and even if you kill me, I just want you to
> remember one thing.

> FAITH
> (lightly)
> What's that, luv?

> WESLEY
> (cold and simple:)
> You are a piece of sh--

Pissed, she stuffs the gag back into Wesley's mouth, pushing it in as far as she can.

>   FAITH
> You should talk. I guess I'll just have to try a
> little harder.

She crosses to a table. Picks up a framed photograph.

Faith looks at the photo for a beat, then slams it down on the table. Shattering the glass.

When she turns back around to Wesley, she's holding a very long SHARD OF BROKEN GLASS.

>   FAITH (cont'd)
> We'll switch to Sharp for awhile.

Off Wesley --

34 INT. CORDELIA'S APARTMENT - NIGHT   34

Cordelia, bandage on her head or wet rag held to it, has papers spread on the table. All the research that she and Wesley had gathered. And a map of downtown L.A.

>   CORDELIA
> (pointing at map)
> ... on Monday a guy was beaten up here, his wallet
> and car were stolen - he's still in the hospital -
> four blocks over is the bar where they had a major
> knock down drag out on Tuesday; then here another
> guy ran into something he referred to as the bitch
> from hell who sent him home- with paramedics. That
> was Wednesday. It's kind of like history class when
> you look at the map with a big red arrow showing
> you how the Germans drove into one of those coun-
> tries and smashed and killed everybody.

>   ANGEL
> (looking at map)
> This was the first. Took his wallet and keys.
> (looks at Cordy)
> He's still in the hospital?

>   CORDELIA
> Yeah. We were just gonna go down and talk to him.

>   ANGEL
> Where's he live?

>   CORDELIA
> I think we have it here...
> (starts going through papers)
> ... somewhere.

35 EXT. DOWNTOWN LOFT APARTMENT - NIGHT

HIGH ANGLE next to a building. LIGHT shines from a window above.

One of the loft windows opens and we SEE FAITH leaning into the night air. Breathing in the coolness for a moment. She holds out her hand.

INSERT - FAITH'S HAND

holding the shard of glass. But the glass is not clear anymore,

FROM AN ANGLE LOOKING UP AT FAITH'S HAND, with Faith framed in the window
behind, she lets the glass fall from her fingers. THE BROKEN PIECE OF GLASS
tumbles past US IN SLOW MOTION.

36 INT. DOWNTOWN LOFT APARTMENT - NIGHT
Faith turns back from the window, refreshed.

                    FAITH
          That's refreshing. But I'm feeling a little cold
          now. What d'you say we warm the place up.

Faith crosses the room.

Wesley, gag in his mouth again, watches Faith. He is tired. His shirt has
been cut open. We can't see exactly where he's been cut, but his white shirt
has soaked up streaks of blood.

Faith rummages around in the kitchen area of the loft.

                    FAITH (cont'd)
          Do you ever wonder if things would've been different
          if we'd never met?

Faith turns around, holding a spray can of cooking oil in one hand and
something else in the other.

                    FAITH (cont'd)
          I mean, what if you had Buffy... and Giles had been
          my Watcher. Would we still be here right now? Or
          would Giles be sitting in that chair?

She flicks a lighter in her hand. A little flame glows brightly.

                    FAITH (cont'd)
          Or is it just like Fate and there's no choice and
          you were gonna be here no matter what? You ever
          think about that stuff? Fate and destiny? ...I
          don't.

Then she sprays the oil into the flame. And the OIL IGNITES. Like a small
hand-held flame thrower. She stops the spray. The fire disappears. She
starts toward Wesley.

                    FAITH (cont'd)
          Not that any of this is your own fault, but since
          this may be the last chance we have to unload on
          each other, I feel it's kind of my duty to tell you
          that if you'd been a better Watcher, I might've
          become a more positive role model.

She moves up right next to him.

                    FAITH (cont'd)
          Face it, Wesley, you really were a jerk. Always
          walkin' around like you had a great big stake rammed
          up your English Channel.

She pulls off his gag.

>   FAITH (cont'd)
>   I think I want to hear you scream.
>
>   WESLEY
>   You never will.

She flicks on the lighter. And pushes the spray. The oil bursts into flames right next to Wesley's face.

>   WESLEY (cont'd)
>   There might be a certain amount of whimpering.

Wesley tries to back away. The flames get closer... Wesley strains back... Faith smiles...

>   FAITH
>   Admit it, Wesley... didn't you always have the hots
>   for me?

SHE pushes the FLAME RIGHT UP TO HIM JUST AS...

The door SLAMS OPEN and Angel crashes into the room.

Faith, startled, backs up from Wesley. We can see the anger in Angel's face when he sees what she's done to Wesley.

She immediately drops her little flame thrower as Angel starts toward her. But she comes back with a knife, pressing it against Wesley's throat.

>   FAITH (cont'd)
>   'Bout time, Soul-Boy.
>   You ready to play now?
>
>   ANGEL
>   I'm ready.

BLACK OUT.

                    END OF ACT THREE

                    ACT FOUR

37 INT. DOWNTOWN LOFT APARTMENT - NIGHT

Faith has the knife still pressed against Wesley's throat. Angel has stopped moving toward her. But he's walking around her.

>   FAITH
>   Okay, you showed, but how do I know you're really
>   in this? What if I kill him? Would that help... or
>   just be really funny?

Wesley glances at Angel. Straining to pull back from the blade.

>   ANGEL
>   You think I don't know what you're after.

For the first time we see a crack in Faith's armor. The bravado suddenly seems a little forced.

                        ANGEL (cont'd)
            I do.

She pushes the blade harder into Wesley's throat as if to cover, drawing a
little blood. He winces, glancing at Faith. Her attention is on Angel.

                        FAITH
            You I *have* to kill... Wesley's just for the hell of
            it.

Angel moves around the back of Faith. She doesn't take her eyes off him.

                        ANGEL
            This isn't about Wesley, it's about you and me.

Wesley keeps his eyes on Faith. Watching her every move. His eyes following
her hands.

                        FAITH
            No, baby, he's payback.

                        ANGEL
            For what? I thought you were happy with the way you
            are.
            (beat)
            By the way, you never told me how much I'm worth
            dusted. Just out of curiosity.

                        FAITH
            ...Fifteen thousand, plus expenses.

                        ANGEL
            (offended)
            You're kidding.

                        FAITH
            Hey, I'm young and willing to work my way up.

                        ANGEL
            You feel young, do you Faith? You're lookin' pretty
            worn out to me...

For a moment she hesitates with the knife, his words cutting her -- and
suddenly Wesley kicks back in the chair. Faith loses her grip and Angel
lunges...

WESLEY

crashes to the floor.

ANGEL

slams into Faith. Knocking her back --

KNIFE

-- landing blade down into the wooden floor right next to Wesley's head.

FAITH

is already rolling to her feet as Angel comes at her. WITH TWO STAKES in
hand. She kicks. He blocks, punches her.

She swings a stake at him. He ducks. She swings the other. He dives and rolls, coming up as she leaps at him.

Angel kicks hard, knocking a stake flying across the room. She swings the other at him. But he grabs the stake and jams an elbow into her face. Her head snaps back.

He holds the stake with both hands and swings her around hard. She can't hold on, losing her grip. She slams into the wall.

Angel snaps the stake in half. Throwing it aside...

...as Faith leaps on him, wrapping her legs around his waist and head butting him hard. Then hitting him again and again.

He falls back, dropping to the floor. She rolls off and up, coming back at him. But he's ready.

Angel ducks a blow, spins around and catches her hard across the head. She slams back into a table, knocking it over.

WESLEY

struggles with the ropes on his hands. Straining to get loose. But the ropes hold tight. He looks to the knife. It's his only chance.

ANGEL

Dives at Faith, but she rolls out of the way and is on her feet. She kicks Angel, sending him slamming into a wall.

> FAITH
> That all you got, vampire? <u>Get in the game!</u>

She goes at him hard. He grabs a chair, swings it into her and knocks her sprawling.

WESLEY

Inches his way toward the knife, crawling as best he can on his side, still tied to the chair. He glances at Angel and Faith. He knows that if Faith kills Angel, well... his life expectancy declines rapidly.

And he's a bit depressed when he sees...

FAITH

Kick Angel in the side. She's nearly insane with rage.

> FAITH
> COME ON! I thought you were supposed to be bad!

Then she hits him hard in the face. Angel crashes down.

> FAITH (cont'd)
> 'Cause I'm bad, Angel -- you can't take me --
> (kicks him again)
> -- no one can take me.

She goes for him, but Angel rolls to his feet, blocking Faith's next punch, grabbing her arm and flinging her half way across the room.

Faith slams to the floor and slides across it, crashing into the wall and knocking over stuff.

WESLEY

Is relieved. He maneuvers himself around so his back is to the knife. He
pushes --

HIS HANDS

-- up against the blade. As he feels the ropes against the blade he starts
cutting. But his attention turns to --

FAITH

-- as she gets to her feet right in front of the window, pulling up a
shattered, jagged two foot long piece of WOOD - (shattered table leg?) a
STAKE.

> FAITH
> COME ON!!

Angel CHARGES -- she misses with the stake as he slams into her. They both
crash back through the glass.

38 EXT. LOFT BUILDING - NIGHT

The loft window explodes outward, glass flying, as Angel and Faith crash
through.

FROM A LOW ANGLE Angel and Faith drop right toward us. Slamming down onto a
metal trash bin. Faith losing the stake as she hits hard. They crash into
the--

39 EXT. ALLEY - NIGHT

Both dazed by the fall. Faith gets up. Bleeding from cuts across her face.
Her clothes are torn. She goes after Angel. He's still dazed, struggling to
his feet.

> FAITH
> I'm gonna kill you.

She kicks Angel in the back, sending him slamming into the wall.

40 INT. DOWNTOWN LOFT APARTMENT - NIGHT

Wesley's rope is cut half way through. He's desperately trying to free
himself. Pushing his wrists hard against the blade.

He can HEAR THE FIGHT from the alley below. A body slamming into metal. The
dull thuds of body blows. He can only imagine the horrible injuries they are
inflicting on each other.

41 EXT. ALLEY - NIGHT
Angel turns as Faith hits him in the face, then knees him.

> FAITH
> YOU HEAR ME? You don't know what evil is!

She kicks him in the face. Angel staggers.

> FAITH (cont'd)
> I'M BAD!

Faith kicks Angel again. He drops back, blocking. She charges at him, swinging her fists as fast as she can, pummeling him. She is furious, fighting blindly, just punching and kicking. Completely out of control.

> FAITH (cont'd)
> Fight back!

Angel is taking a brutal beating. But Faith is tiring. She is physically exhausted, emotionally drained.

> FAITH (cont'd)
> You are going to die!

She throws another punch -- but suddenly Angel grabs her fist in mid-punch.

> ANGEL
> Nice try, Faith.

Angel flings her hard. She flies back, crashes into the building or a metal doorway.

Angel goes right after her, unrelenting.

> ANGEL (cont'd)
> I know what you want.

Angel comes at her -- she hits him, he hits her right back, just as hard.

> ANGEL (cont'd)
> And I'm not gonna do it.

42 INT. DOWNTOWN LOFT APARTMENT - NIGHT

Wesley pulls the ropes off his body, works as fast as he can to free his legs.

43 EXT. ALLEY - NIGHT

Faith looks up at Angel through the hair falling across her eyes. And the blood from cuts smearing across her face.

She tries to hit him -- she's getting weak. Angel stares directly into her eyes.

> ANGEL
> I'm not going to make it easy for you.

Faith's expression changes in a flash, from defeat to I'm gonna kill you you motherfucker if it's the last thing I do.

She tries to hit and kick him, crying, sobbing with rage:

> FAITH
> I'M EVIL!

44 INT. DOWNTOWN LOFT APARTMENT - NIGHT

Wesley frantically untangles the ropes, gets to his feet. He's hurt, but that's not going to stop him. He moves to the window.

HIS P.O.V. OF THE ALLEY BELOW

Faith pounding Angel.

WESLEY

Oh shit.

He looks around quickly for a weapon. Maybe yanks open a drawer of utensils, comes up with the knife.

45 EXT. ALLEY - NIGHT

Faith, crying hysterically, beats on Angel (he lets her).

                    FAITH
          You hear me? I'm bad...!

46 EXT. DOWNTOWN LOFT BUILDING - NIGHT

Wesley drops down onto the trash bin, slams into the alley. But comes up with the look of a killer, with a LARGE KITCHEN KNIFE IN HAND. Despite his injuries, he's remarkably adept. Not fumbling. But... heroic.

HIS P.O.V. DOWN THE ALLEY

In the shadows he can make out two dark figures. And one is getting up.

WESLEY

Starts running toward them.

47 EXT. ALLEY - NIGHT

Faith screams at Angel:

                    FAITH
          I'M BAD!

Then she cracks, she can't take anymore. She may fall to her knees or wind up crouched on the ground or not, depending on how the scene feels at this point. She may crack and say the tiny voiced "I'm bad" without him holding her -- see how it plays.

Angel grabs her arms and holds her tight. She's staring at him, crying and bleeding and broken -- and now, in a tiny voice, almost that of a child's:

                    FAITH (cont'd)
          ... I'm bad. Angel... I'm bad... Just do it...
          please. Just kill me...

Faith finally collapses. Angel holds her.

WESLEY

Runs down the alley toward them... but when he realizes that Angel is holding her... he slows down... is she dead? No... we can HEAR SOMEONE CRYING. Angel, crying? MAYBE BECAUSE SHE'S DEAD. No... IT'S A WOMAN CRYING.... It's Faith...

Wesley steps closer. He pulls off his glasses, just to make sure. Stunned by what he sees.

ANGEL

Holding Faith in his arms. And her sobbing like... a real person.

SLOW MOTION - THE KNIFE

Drops from Wesley's hand.

HIGH ANGLE SHOT OF THE ALLEY

Wesley standing in the alley. Angel holding Faith.

And her arms slowly lift up and hold onto Angel.

48 EXT. ALLEY - RUMANIA - NIGHT (FLASHBACK)

CAMERA PUSHES towards the darkness of the now familiar alley. We may see man who was flung into street still lying unconscious in it. We may also see First Man stirring in the alley.

Angel staggers out, in normal face, breathing hard, just as tormented as we've ever seen him.

Hold him for a beat. PUSHING PAST him until we find the woman he attacked. She is breathing hard, too, and more than a little surprised to find herself alive.

She lowers her hand from her neck, revealing the two bite marks and the bit of blood running down.

HER P.O.V. OF ANGEL

STAGGERING AWAY FROM HER into the night.

CLOSE ON ANGEL

As he leans back a wall, breathing hard. A look of panic... something has happened to him... and he's the one that is now terrified. He closes his eyes, fighting back a fear that he can't define, then he pushes away from the wall. And heads off into the night. Perhaps a matching cut to:

49 EXT. COUNTRYSIDE - LONG SHOT - NIGHT

LEAFLESS trees outlined against an almost surreal moonlit nightscape... ALMOST DEVOID OF ANY COLOR. Giving us the feeling that nothing is alive in this land... except the lone figure of a man walking aimlessly to nowhere.

BLACK OUT.

<u>THE END</u>

ANGEL
"Five by Five"

SET LIST INTERIORS

BUS DEPOT GARAGE
DARLA'S HOUSE (FLASHBACK)
       KITCHEN
       LIVING ROOM
ANGEL'S BUILDING
       INNER OFFICE
       OUTER OFFICE
       APARTMENT
BAR
COURTROOM
WOLFRAM & HART BUILDING
       LINDSEY'S OFFICE
       LOBBY
GOVERNMENT BUILDING ROTUNDA
CORDELIA'S APARTMENT
       HALL
       BEDROOM
DOWNTOWN LOFT APARTMENT

EXTERIORS

DOWNTOWN
UNDER THE BRIDGE
STREET
BAR - NIGHT (STOCK)
ANOTHER BAR
LOS ANGELES SKYLINE - DAY (STOCK)
WOLFRAM & HART BUILDING - NIGHT (STOCK)
ROMANIAN ALLEY (FLASHBACK)
ROMANIAN STREET (FLASHBACK)
DOWNTOWN LOFT APARTMENT
ALLEY
COUNTRYSIDE

ANGEL™

PHOTO COVER GALLERY

ANGEL

issue one

scriptbook

Episode
CITY OF

Written By
JOSS WHEDON & DAVID GREENWALT

ANGEL

issue two

scriptbook

™

Episode
A HOLE IN THE WORLD

Written By
JOSS WHEDON

ANGEL

issue three

scriptbook

Episode
SPIN THE BOTTLE

Written By
JOSS WHEDON

ANGEL

issue four   scriptbook ™

Episode
WAITING IN THE WINGS

Written By
JOSS WHEDON

ANGEL

issue five

scriptbook

Episode
Five by Five

Written By
JIM KOUF

www.IDWPUBLISHING.com